CRITICAL CURRICULUM STUDIES

Critical Curriculum Studies: Education, Consciousness, and the Politics of Knowing offers a novel framework for thinking about how curriculum relates to students' understanding of the world around them. Wayne Au brings together curriculum theory, critical educational studies, and feminist standpoint theory with practical examples of teaching for social justice to argue for a transformative curriculum that challenges existing inequity in social, educational, and economic relations. Making use of the work of important scholars such as Freire, Vygotsky, Hartsock, Harding, and others, *Critical Curriculum Studies*, argues that we must understand the relationship between the curriculum and the types of consciousness we carry out into the world.

Wayne Au is an assistant professor in the Education Program at the University of Washington, Bothell Campus and is an editor for the social justice education magazine, *Rethinking Schools*.

CRITICAL CURRICULUM STUDIES

Education, Consciousness, and the Politics of Knowing

Wayne Au

Routledge
Taylor & Francis Group

NEW YORK AND LONDON

First published 2012
by Routledge
711 Third Avenue, New York, NY 10017

Simultaneously published in the UK
by Routledge
2 Park Square, Milton Park, Abingdon, Oxon OX14 4RN

Routledge is an imprint of the Taylor & Francis Group, an informa business

Library of Congress Cataloging in Publication Data
Au, Wayne, 1972-
Critical curriculum studies : education, consciousness, and the politics of
knowing / Wayne Au.
p. cm. – (Critical social thought series)
Includes bibliographical references and index.
1. Education–Curricula–Social aspects–United States. 2. Transformative
learning–Curricula–United States. 3. Critical pedagogy–United States. I. Title.
LB1570.A93 2011
370.11'5–dc22
2011005934

ISBN: 978-0-415-87711-4 (hbk)
ISBN: 978-0-415-87712-1 (pbk)
ISBN: 978-0-203-80644-9 (ebk)

Typeset in Bembo
by Taylor & Francis Books

Dedicated to Makoto Choge Shimabukuro-Au
Son, you have taught me more about love and
living and learning than I ever imagined possible.

CONTENTS

ACKNOWLEDGMENTS

This volume would not have been possible without the political, intellectual, emotional, and personal support of a whole bunch of folks (mostly in no particular order):

Benji Chang, Kristen Buras, Michael Dumas, Jeff Sapp (and Sino and Helena), Eugene Fujimoto, Nga Wing Wong, the Kuma Krew, Diana Hess, Luis Gandin, Linda Mizell, Jesse Hagopian, Sarah McFarlane, Ken Rubin, Michael Vavrus, Katy Swalwell, Paulette Thompson, Taina Rosario-Collazo, Katie Baydo-Reed, Bill Ayers, Christine Sleeter, Antonia Darder, Peter McLaren, Anthony Brown, Kefferlyn Brown, Sonia Nieto, Bree Picower, Karen Zapata, Dave Stovall, Brian Gibbs, and Rima Apple.

My former colleagues at CSU Fullerton, especially Mark Ellis, Kristin Stang, Debbie Ambrosetti, Daniel Choi, Pablo Jasis, Nick Henning, and the Researchers And Critical Educators (RACE) group.

My current colleagues at the University of Washington, especially Brad Portin and Cherry Banks for the opportunity to teach at UW Bothell and return home to Seattle, as well as Walter Parker, Ken Zeichner, James Banks, and Ed Taylor for their ongoing support.

My comrades at *Rethinking Schools* past and present—Bob Peterson, Linda Christensen, Stan Karp, Bill Bigelow, Melissa Tempel, Stephanie Walters, Kelley Dawson-Salas, Rita Tenorio, Mike Trokan, Teagan Dowling, Jody Sokolower, Kathy Xiong, Dyan Watson, Helen Gym, Barbara Miner, Catherine Capellaro, Fred McKissack, Hyung Nam, and David Levine.

Special thanks to those who've read parts or all of this manuscript (in various versions) and provided much needed, critical feedback: Thomas Thomas, Noah DeLissovoy, Keita Takayama, Minerva Chavez, Alexa Dimick, Joe Ferrare, Rosie Ordonez-Jasis, and my dear friend, mentor, and colleague, Michael W. Apple.

Also thanks to Catherine Bernard and Georgette Enriquez at Routledge for their ongoing support of my work.

My entire family (the Aus, Shimabukuros, Welles, Colungas, Itos, DeWeeses, DeWeese-Parkinsons), but especially my father-in-law Bob, my mother Priscilla, and my mother-in-law Cathie for providing childcare (which helped me carve out time to write), as well as Veronica Barrera, Chiloé Barrera-Chloyd, and Yume Barrera-Matsudaira for the continued love and support.

This book would also not have happened without the love of my life, Mira Shimabukuro. Thank you.

Of course, any and all shortcomings are mine and mine alone.

Portions of *Critical Curriculum Studies* have appeared in:

Au, W. (2010). Critical reflection in the classroom: Over-determination, relative autonomy, and consciousness in social studies education. In A. DeLeon & E. W. Ross, (Eds.), *Critical theories, radical pedagogies, and social education: Towards new perspectives for social studies education* (pp. 163–82). Amsterdam: Sense Publishers.

Au, W. (2011). Critical standpoint in the curriculum: Challenging hegemony in the politics of knowledge. In Malott, C. S. & Porfilio, B. J. (Eds.), *Critical pedagogy in the 21st century: A new generation of scholars* (pp. 213–32). Charlotte, NC: Information Age Publishers.

SERIES EDITOR INTRODUCTION

In the midst of the Depression of the 1930s, George Counts challenged educators with a crucial question. Can the school contribute to building a new and more equal society? For Counts, the answer was yes, if and only if educators took up their responsibility to challenge dominant economic, political, and cultural relations (Counts, 1932). Counts of course was not alone in raising this question. Educators such as Harold Rugg, Theodore Brameld, and others joined him. W. E. B. DuBois, Carter G. Woodson, and Anna Julia Cooper as well spoke eloquently about the realities of oppressed peoples and the place of education in the ongoing struggles to overcome dominance (see, e.g., Lewis, 2000; Woodson, 1933/1990). Similar powerful voices could be found among other minoritized groups and were ever present among women activists.

The distressing conditions from which these voices emerged are strikingly visible again today. Impoverishment, unemployment, and growing inequalities are coupled with a neoliberal and neoconservative agenda that once more defends the economic and political arrangements that led to the crisis in the first place. In education, an emphasis on privatization, competition, test-driven curriculum, an attack on teachers and serious multiculturalisms, and so much more mirrors this agenda (Apple, 2006). In many ways, we are witnessing the 1930s all over again.

Like the 1930s, committed educators are again faced with the pressing issues surrounding what schools can do to challenge what is happening in the larger society and to prepare their students to understand and act as critical citizens in that society. We are once again called upon to re-engage with issues that simply will not go away, that cannot be easily solved using our usual technical models of reasoning. What counts as "official knowledge"? What social goals should guide our decisions? Who should make curricular decisions? What is the relationship between our answers to these questions and the kind of socially just society we want for ourselves and our children (see Apple, 2000; 2004)?

A key element in all of these questions is the curriculum itself. The concept of curriculum by its very nature cannot be neutral. It is fundamentally valuative. It involves what Raymond Williams so felicitously called the "selective tradition"—someone's knowledge, someone's ideas about what counts as legitimate culture (Williams, 1961). Discussions of curriculum, hence, lie at the very heart of any serious consideration of education and the values that underpin it.

One would think then that the curriculum field, a field with a very long history of dealing with such issues (Kliebard, 2004), would be at the center of these important public debates. Unfortunately, for much of the field this is not the case. It is as if we have cut ourselves off from the rich traditions of the field in actually dealing with the selection and teaching of the actual stuff of the curriculum and with the conceptual, political, policy related, and practical concerns involved in this. Because of this, a good deal of the literature in the curriculum field is rhetorical. It substitutes slogans for detailed conceptual, historical, and empirical work. Furthermore, too much of it has all too often lost any real connections with the realities of what happens in classrooms.

The literature in critical curriculum studies has not been immune from these problems. Here too, political slogans too often reign supreme. Not enough thought is given to the realities of teachers' and administrators' lives, to the actual power relations and problems they face everyday, and to discussions and depictions of short term and long term tactics of what can be done in the face of these realities (see, e.g., Apple & Beane, 2007; Apple, Au, & Gandin, 2009). At the same time, insufficient attention is given to building a rich conceptual and empirical foundation of actually doing critical curriculum work in a truly disciplined manner.

This is where Wayne Au enters. He raises serious questions about a number of the current tendencies within the curriculum field. He provides a set of theoretical principles for thinking more rigorously about critical curriculum work. He grounds these principles in a rich international literature on dialectical forms of reasoning. This in itself would be a very thoughtful contribution. But *Critical Curriculum Studies* is not only a significant conceptual contribution. Au provides detailed examples of what a critically oriented practice actually looks like.

In his well-received earlier book, *Unequal by Design* (Au, 2009), Wayne Au offered a devastating indictment of the over-emphasis on standardized high stakes testing and reductive forms of accountability in education. In that book, he pointed out how such policies reduce curriculum to simplistic facts to be mastered for simplistic tests and reduce students and teachers to answer-producing machines. Au now turns to a set of issues that arise from this indictment. He asks us to think in a truly radical manner about alternative (perhaps *oppositional* is a better word here) ways of engaging in education.

One of the most important magazines that consistently publish interesting material in critical education is *Rethinking Schools*. Wayne Au is one of the editors of *Rethinking Schools* and in this role has published a number of important pieces in it on critical multicultural education, on testing, and other topics. His credentials as someone who can link the complex politics involved in educational policy with the daily struggles of building and defending an education that is worthy of its name are unquestionable. In *Critical Curriculum Studies*, Au uses his skills in bringing together issues of theory, policies, and practice in important ways. He takes up the ambitious project of asking and answering fundamental questions in curriculum. Among these are: What are the theoretical and epistemological foundations of critical curriculum studies? How should we think about the relationship among society, knowledge, and persons in more nuanced ways? What do these more nuanced understandings bring to curriculum theory and curriculum design? What are the concrete practices that embody these critical understandings?

In her very thoughtful book *The Social Production of Art* (Wolff, 1984), Janet Wolff reminds us that even our most creative forms of knowledge are *socially* rooted and depend on an entire assemblage of social processes and collective forms of knowing and making. Wayne Au's understanding of knowledge and his social rootedness is very similar to this. He argues for and then provides us with a detailed depiction of a more dialectical understanding of consciousness—a key concept in thinking critically about the relationship between knowers and knowledge. By drawing on a profoundly social conception of consciousness, he is able to reassert more collective understandings of the ways in which people construct their realities and how their knowledge is connected to those realities in dynamic ways.

This has crucial significance for how we think about curriculum and for how we design environments so that students can learn existing knowledge and produce new knowledge that gives them power in the larger society. And it relates directly to the position on curriculum that is taken in this book, for Au is articulate in building and defending a position on curriculum that sees it as a process of *environmental design*. The environment, the knower(s), the known, and the to-be-known, and how we are to think about all of this—all interconnected dialectically and socially—these are key elements in the conception of curriculum that Au presents. Though more politically engaged than some of the historical figures who held similar beliefs about the curriculum, this connects him to a long tradition that includes Dewey and more recently Huebner and myself. It is a history that needs to be continually recaptured and lived.

Critical Curriculum Studies is a provocative book. It challenges many of our assumptions about curriculum, including a number of the assumptions held by politically progressive and critical curriculum scholars as well. This is as it should be. The word "critical" implies serious deliberations and debates over what a field takes for granted. Au rightly asks us to engage in such debates over our politics, theories, policies, and practices. Given the realities of this society, this is a crucial task.

Michael W. Apple
John Bascom Professor of Curriculum and Instruction
and Educational Policy Studies
University of Wisconsin, Madison

References

Apple, M. W. (2000). *Official knowledge: Democratic education in a conservative age*, 2nd ed. New York: Routledge.

Apple, M. W. (2004). *Ideology and curriculum*, 3rd ed. New York: Routledge.

Apple, M. W. (2006). *Educating the "right" way: Markets, standards, God, and inequality*, 2nd ed. New York: Routledge.

Apple, M. W., Au, W., & Gandin, L. A. (Eds.) (2009). *The Routledge international handbook of critical education*. New York: Routledge.

Apple, M. W. & Beane, J. A. (Eds.) (2007). *Democratic schools: Lessons in powerful education*, 2nd ed. Portsmouth, NH: Heinemann.

Au, W. (2009). *Unequal by design: High-stakes testing and the standardization of inequality*. New York: Routledge.

Counts, G. S. (1932). *Dare the school build a new social order?* New York: John Day Company.

Kliebard, H. M. (2004). *The struggle for the American curriculum*, 3rd ed. New York: Routledge Falmer.

Lewis, D. L. (2000). *W. E. B. Du Bois: The fight for equality and the American century, 1919–1963*. New York: Henry Holt.

Williams, R. (1961). *The long revolution*. London: Chatto & Windus.

Wolff, J. (1984). *The social production of art*. New York: New York University Press.

Woodson, C. G. (1933/1990). *The mis-education of the negro*. Trenton: Africa World Press.

1

INTRODUCTION: CONTRADICTION IN CURRICULUM STUDIES

My career as a credentialed social studies and language arts teacher began at Middle College High School at South Seattle Community College. Housed on the community college campus, Middle College was a small, alternative Seattle public high school for former dropouts, ages 16–21—"former" because these students had dropped out (or, more correctly, had been pushed out) of the regular high schools but realized that they wanted another chance at graduating and getting their diploma. This was the job I wanted, and I loved teaching there. My students hailed from the vastly diverse, working class families of South Seattle and the overwhelming majority were always on the brink of crisis: the brink of being in a gang, or dealing drugs, or some street life related hustle; the brink of homelessness or unemployment; the brink of drug and alcohol abuse; the brink of depression or suicide; the brink of going to jail; the brink of serious health issues. And sometimes we lost students to these crises, over the brink, never to return.

I don't intend to sound overly dire here, but this was (and is) the reality of an increasing number of our students' lives. As of 2009, for instance, even though they make up only 25 percent of the overall population, 42 percent (31.3 million) of the children in the United States live in low income families, (Chau, Thampi, & Wight, 2010), and it is fairly well established that poverty-related issues such as food insecurity and lack of adequate health care negatively impact educational success (Berliner, 2009). As a school for "dropouts," we had a high concentration of students dealing with serious issues.

Even in the midst of such struggles, though, our students were also always on the brink of educational success as they fought off the demons of self-doubt and low skills in order to graduate. And they were brilliant, passionate, and artistic, often culturally and politically aware and certainly, in some regards, wizened well beyond their years. As I said before, I loved working with those students. They were feisty, wouldn't tolerate bullshit, lived passionately, had wickedly sharp intellects and humor, and embodied so much potential to transform their own lives—especially if they found the wherewithal to fight against the material constraints so present in their daily lives. When our students finished, everyone had serious reason to celebrate, so there was nothing quite like the joyous experience of a Middle College High School Graduation.

In addition to having left their traditional high schools, my Middle College students had at least one other thing in common: As they pretty much hated the education they experienced before landing in our program, they were alienated from schools. Emotionally, academically, culturally, socially, politically, and sometimes even physically scarred by the "regular" system of education, my students all had what one might call PTSD: Post Traumatic Schooling Disorder. Such extreme alienation was what we tried to overcome at Middle College, and while we did not always succeed (e.g., our attrition hovered around losing 1/3 of our students each quarter, usually either due to a lack of maturity or to a poverty-related life event that became too large an obstacle), we worked hard to create a learning environment where students could re-claim their education. In retrospect, I think that overcoming this alienation was the key factor to whatever successes we enjoyed, and we made use of two key strategies to do so. First, on most days and in a multiplicity of ways, we clearly demonstrated that we cared for the well-being of our students on emotional, social, physical, and educational levels. Second, my co-teacher and I developed a culture of curricular resistance in our social studies/language arts coordinated studies class.

The premise of our curricular resistance was simple: We operated from the basic assumption that certain, more politically critical perspectives of the world and the realities of social and historical relations had either been explicitly or implicitly denied our students in their previous education. This approach helped us overcome our students' built-in alienation and resistance to education because it validated their experiences with and feelings about previous curriculum that did not connect to their lives. At the same time our critical curriculum acknowledged and explained what they saw happening in their communities and the world. Building from this assumption (one we explicitly told them was the basis of our teaching), we then sought to develop a curriculum that recognized our students' social, cultural, and economic material realities, one that validated their experiences with the power relations in their lives.

In practice this culture of curricular resistance meant that, for instance, when we taught U.S. history, we used Zinn's (1995) *A People's History of the United States*, which provides the oft-neglected perspectives of many oppressed or marginalized groups in U.S. history. Or when we taught world history, we included books like Galeano's (1998) *Open Veins of Latin America*, which details the European colonization of the Americas, but places a high value on honoring the perspective and resistance of indigenous peoples. Or, when the World Trade Organization met in Seattle in 1999, we engaged in a quarter long study of globalization that paid particular attention to issues of economic exploitation in the global South, theft of indigenous and local knowledge of plants and farming, the environmental ramifications of neoliberal free trade, and forms of resistance to neoliberalism that were manifesting around the world. As a result, our students produced a magazine about the World Trade Organization and many decided to take part in the protests that year (Au, 2000). What unites all of these examples is that through them we developed curriculum that spoke to the foundations of racism, sexism/patriarchy, and class exploitation in this country, curriculum that also pushed students to sharpen their thinking, writing, and critical literacy skills. In many ways, by functionally using what might be referred to, calling upon Freire (1974), as the "curriculum of the oppressed," we made use of students' social locations, lived experiences, and material realities, as a means for them to critically engage with both the world and academic knowledge and skills. Thus this curriculum encouraged students to develop the skills to better understand the systematic relationships that impinged on their very existence, with the hope that they would apply their learning to take control of their own lives by at least graduating and, perhaps, moving into the world as agents of social change too.

Critical Curriculum Studies grows directly out of these experiences teaching at Middle College High School. As a practicing K–12 teacher, I knew what we were teaching worked to reach our students, students typically labeled hard to reach. And while at the time I already had some theoretical and political tools to think about our curriculum and its effectiveness (e.g., some initial contact with the work of Freire through my teacher education program, as well as a personal upbringing on Marxism), I had neither the training nor the time/resources to formally think through the "why" and the "how" our curriculum was so successful with our students.

Now, over 10 years, a Ph.D., and a tenure track university position later, I've finally returned to reflect upon the kinds of curriculum we taught at Middle College—through this book. *Critical Curriculum Studies*, however, is not about my Middle College experiences directly, but the general issues surrounding the politics of the curriculum. Regardless, the arguments and analyses I make here regarding the explanatory power of taking up the standpoint of the oppressed in our teaching are indeed indebted to the students, school, colleagues, and curriculum that launched me as a teacher. *Critical Curriculum Studies*, in addition to its conceptual origins in the context of my past practice, must also be contextualized within curriculum studies as well because, fundamentally, in undertaking this work I am entering into several long-standing debates and controversies in the field. In the next section I take up these issues.

The Crisis in Curriculum Studies

It has been over 40 years since Schwab (1969) declared the field of curriculum studies "moribund," and over 30 years since Huebner (1976) pronounced it "dead." Both scholars made their terminal prognosis based on the same set of symptoms: A perceived conceptual disunity and lack of practical application of curriculum studies to school practices. The field's death has been long and slow, however, as contemporary curriculum scholars regularly express grave concern over conceptual disunity in the field in the intervening years (Jackson, 1996; Morrison, 2004; Wraga & Hlebowitsh, 2003). As such, the scholarly consensus seems to be that curriculum studies is mired in a crisis of disarray and conceptual confusion that inhibits its growth and development (Miller, 2005; Slabbert & Hattingh, 2006).With this volume I seek to enter this ongoing scholarly debate within curriculum studies with the intent of offering one potential conceptual resolution to the self-described crisis in the field. I began this introductory chapter with a recounting of the personal and curricular origins of *Critical Curriculum Studies*. In what follows below, I discuss the current contours of conceptual struggle within the field, a struggle that revolves around what has been constructed as a lack of paradigmatic unity (due to a focus on subjectivities) versus a lack of pragmatic connection to real world curricular issues (due to an over emphasis on theory). I then offer a critical analysis of some of the strengths and weaknesses found within this struggle—all of which serves to set the frame for the overall analysis done here. I follow with an argument about the justification and importance of studying curriculum, as well as a brief overview/ preview of the chapters and arguments of this book. Finally I conclude this chapter with a brief explanation of my own social location and biography as part of a commitment to try to be internally consistent with the epistemological, methodological, and political commitments of *Critical Curriculum Studies* itself.

The Critical Turn in Curriculum Studies

In the mid-1970s, curriculum studies took a notable turn towards critical politics, with issues of equality and power within education highlighted as a focus in curricular research (see, e.g., Anyon, 1980; Apple, 1973, 1975; Rosenbaum, 1976). Pinar (1975, 1978) proclaimed this critical turn as one part of the new chapter in the field of curriculum studies he dubbed the "reconceptualization"—a problematic category that many scholars that Pinar identified as "reconceptualist" fundamentally rejected for being ahistorical and not adequately representing the full range of their work (Apple, 2010b). In the four decades since, a significant number of critical curriculum scholars have developed research trajectories that use postmodernist-influenced theoretical orientations with the expressed intent of explicitly examining the positionality and subjectivity of both knowledge and educational actors (Kafala & Cary, 2006; Slattery, 2006). Specifically, to lesser and greater degrees, scholars have taken up postmodernist-influenced lenses such as feminism (see, e.g., Luke & Gore, 1992), cultural studies (see, e.g., Pinar, 2006), post-structuralism (see, e.g., Popkewitz & Fendler, 1999), disability studies (Erevelles, 2005), neo-Marxism (see, e.g., Apple, 1995), and post-colonial studies (see, e.g., Dimitriadis & McCarthy, 2001), among others, to analyze the politics of school knowledge and classroom practices. While some of the curricular scholarship associated with these analyses maintained an overall focus on material reality (see, e.g., Anyon, 1980; Apple, 1995), what unites

these postmodernist-influenced orientations is an overt recognition of the subjectivity of experience and epistemology (Benton & Craib, 2001) that acknowledges
the complexity of social and material reality for multiple groups and communities
(Fraser, 1995; Hartsock, 1998a). As such, critical scholarship in curriculum studies
has made great strides in not only questioning relationships of power as they
exist within school knowledge, but also in striving for curriculum that is more
equitable, more inclusive of various perspectives, and more resistant to status quo
relations.

Research on synoptic curriculum studies texts confirms a steady shift towards
critical politics in the field (Kim & Marshall, 2006), such that, as Miller (2005) asserts:

> [I]t now certainly is commonplace to view US curriculum studies as situated,
> always located within larger discursive frameworks, always part of US cultural,
> political, and educational moments of the day and place. American curriculum
> studies and curriculum design and development are seen as bound up in a
> wealth of local political, cultural, economic, social, historical complexities.
> Curriculum is taken as embedded in multiple local contexts of use, multiple
> contexts of construction and relationships.
>
> *(p. 18)*

Thus, between postmodernism's focus on the subjectivity of meaning and perspective
(Benton & Craib, 2001), the increased presence of post-modern influenced critical
theories in curriculum studies (Kim & Marshall, 2006; Miller, 2005), and the fragmented
and compartmentalized structures of schooling and curriculum generally (Slabbert &
Hattingh, 2006), the existence of a fractured or balkanized field of curriculum studies
should be hardly surprising (Kafala & Cary, 2006; Säfström, 1999): Scholars have
been applying new paradigms and epistemologies in their attempts to more fully
understand the complexity of what is taught in schools as well as the meanings that
students, teachers, and communities subsequently construct in the process.

The Pragmatic Response

The shift towards analyses that explicitly focused on politics and power in school
knowledge did not happen without resistance within curriculum studies. Weighing
in on both the death of the field and the then recent critical turn, Jackson (1980)
disagreed with both Schwab's (1969) and Huebner's (1976) prognoses and asserted
that perhaps the field of curriculum studies never really existed, going on to deride
the rise of critical politics in the field. Hlebowitsh (1993, 1997, 1999, 2005) and
Wraga (1998, 1999; Wraga & Hlebowitsh, 2003) have carried forward aspects of
Jackson's critique into more contemporary scholarly debates by asserting that the
field of curriculum studies has given too much credence to critical theorizing, and
in turn has over-politicized the field, focused too much on theoretical exploration,
and neglected practical curriculum design.

In specific response to the critical turn in curriculum studies, Wraga and Hlebowitsh (2003) call for a "renaissance" in curriculum theory that specifically rejects critical paradigmatic orientations that they suggest have no place in the field, where ideology and "sound scholarship" are incompatible and where life experience should not be considered within the curriculum. Thus they fundamentally advocate for a de-politicized field where "curriculum scholars shed ideological blinders, clearly delineate boundaries of the field, consciously build upon the field's constructive legacies, and foster a robust interplay between curriculum theory and curriculum practice" (p. 435).

There are three aspects of Wraga and Hlebowitsh's (2003) framing that are particularly important to highlight. First is their lamentation that curriculum studies does not have the same amount of power or effectiveness that it once leveraged in schools in the United States. Their renaissance thus hints at a return to a romantic past where districts and schools relied on university scholarship for curricular guidance. Second, and fundamental to their overall analysis, is a pragmatic push for curriculum studies to embrace school practice. This aspect serves the dual purposes of critiquing critical scholars for being focused on theory as well as increasing the relevance of the field in the day-to-day operations of schools. Third, and as an extension of their pragmatism, is their idea that by focusing more on practice (what works and what needs to be done), curriculum studies necessarily should not incorporate ideology, politics, personal experience, culture, and other forms of subjectivity that might be brought to analyses of school knowledge.

Pragmatic and Subjective Considerations

Despite the strengths offered by postmodern subjectivity in recognizing the centrality of identity and context in curriculum studies, as well as the concrete practicality called for by curricular pragmatists, both positions suffer from some critical shortcomings. For instance, Wraga and Hlebowitsh's (2003) suggested curricular "renaissance" is extremely problematic. Most prominent is their push to focus on issues other than the existence of political, cultural, and ideological relationships between schools, the curriculum, and society—a position that seems questionable considering the sheer amount of empirical research that points to the centrality of such relationships to all aspects of the curriculum (see, e.g., Apple, 2004, 2006; Au, 2009f). The boundaries of our knowledge, including what comes to "count" as legitimate curricular knowledge, are intimately intertwined with social and political relations (Apple, 2000; Bernstein, 1999; Buras, 2008; Cornbleth & Waugh, 1995). Further, it seems equally impossible to deny the ideological nature of *all* scholarship and research (Canagarajah, 2002; Harding, 2004a; Sandoval, 2000), particularly when researchers themselves lay claim to ideological neutrality and, by extension, methodological objectivity, associated with the positivistic sciences (Benton & Craib, 2001). In this regard, Wraga and Hlebowitsh's (2003) call for curriculum studies to "shed ideological blinders" (p. 435) in search of some form of paradigmatic unity lends itself to a hegemonically defined field of curriculum studies (Morrison, 2004), one based more on positivistic epistemologies. In this sense Wraga and Hlebowitsh's (2003) response to critical subjectivity in curriculum studies implies a call for a form of hegemonic normative pragmatism.

It is important to recognize that there is nothing inherently negative about the growth of criticality in curriculum studies, just as there is nothing inherently negative about a lack of paradigmatic unity in the field (Säfström, 1999). Indeed, one could argue that the diverse forms of critical analyses demonstrate the field's resilience, strength, and adaptability. Further, given the conservative modernization that has taken place socially and educationally (Apple, 2006) and the increasing institutional inequalities both nationally and internationally associated with neoliberal globalization (Lipman, 2004; McLaren & Farahmandpur, 2005), the critical turn in curriculum studies seems more than appropriate. Further still, the modern decline in the influence of curriculum studies in public education must be understood within the current context, particularly the shifting and diverse stakeholders involved in public school reform (Burch, 2009; Pinar, 1999), the evolving systems of state governance and the role that education plays in that evolution (Ball, 2003a; Clarke & Newman, 1997), and the increasing influence of tests and textbook publishers on the curriculum (Au, 2007b, 2009f).

Despite the above criticisms, it is equally important to acknowledge an important issue within curriculum studies that Wraga and Hlebowitsh (2003) correctly identify: Curriculum studies would be better served if it were more grounded in schools and met the concrete needs of practicing teachers (Apple, 2010a). Likewise, curriculum studies could also be more relevant if one of its goals was to highlight the relationship between theory and practice in ways that would appeal to practicing teachers as well. In their assessment, however, Wraga and Hlebowitsh (2003) flatly charge critical curriculum scholars with being particularly disconnected from actual curricular practice at the school and classroom level. On one level such an assessment makes sense given that critical scholarship tends to interrogate problems and can thus be guilty of not providing pragmatic solutions for teachers. On another level, however, such an assessment is also problematic because a significant body of the work done by such scholars specifically takes as its focus the politics of power and culture as it manifests in school knowledge at many levels, including the classroom (see, e.g., Anyon, 1980; Apple, 1986, 1995; Beyer & Liston, 1996; Sleeter, 2002). Indeed, the point of much critical scholarship in curriculum studies is to influence practice by taking up real world issues such as educational inequality as a focus.

Intent, however, does not always equate with outcome, and despite the focus of some scholars on practice, it is true that the subjectivity associated with postmodern analyses can often lead to an epistemological disconnection from material reality (Au & Apple, 2009b). While it is absolutely necessary to recognize the crucial role that postmodernist analyses have played in challenging master narratives and injecting the lived experiences of peoples and cultures into all of our work (Apple & Whitty, 2002; Lather, 1992), a difficulty arises due to postmodernism's general rejection of a material world outside of human perception and subjectivity (Bhaskar, 1989; Perry, 2002). Such a position in reaction to the hegemony of positivist sciences is understandable, but fundamentally it negates our ability to change material and social conditions, because within the postmodern epistemological-philosophical paradigm we can never establish that those conditions—whether socially just or unjust— actually exist. It all becomes a matter of perception, or in the case of curriculum studies, a matter of language, discourse, and pure theorizing (Apple, 2010a).

As such, curricularists may have lost the connection between curriculum studies and the material world (Apple, 2010a). It is thus important to re-evaluate the influence of postmodern subjectivity in curriculum studies (Apple, 2010a; Beyer & Liston, 1992, 1996). On this issue, Beyer and Liston (1996) comment:

> For postmodernists, then, without some sense of words and referents that extend beyond the signifier and signified, their talk amounts to nothing or, if it does indeed amount to something, it undermines their own position. Without the possibility of utterances referring to something outside themselves, post-modernism is locked within a circular narcissism, which undermines not only the claims of modernists but postmodern writing as well. Such circularity is debilitating for those involved in education, who are confronted daily with choices that call for concrete action and that often carry long-lasting consequences.
>
> *(p. 150)*

It follows that, while critical curriculum scholars embraced postmodernist subjectivity to lesser and greater degrees (and with lesser and greater effect), a disassociation from material reality is a serious consideration philosophically, epistemologically, and methodologically when post-modernism is brought to bear in any field or discipline (Au & Apple, 2009b).

Between Pragmatism and Subjectivity

Despite my criticisms, it follows that, like Wraga and Hlebowitsh (2003), I too wish to see a heightened focus on practice in curriculum studies, but not for the same reasons. Where they critique critical scholars for focusing on theory (a far too simple assessment, as I argued above), I see curriculum studies as no different than the rest of social science research generally, which historically has struggled with connecting research with reality (Benton & Craib, 2001). Further, Wraga and Hlebowitsh's clarion call for more attention to practice without "ideological blinders" seemingly implies that the study of curriculum should exist in pragmatic isolation from the world, so that our study of it can similarly share in what one might see as the positivist guise of objective, ideologically neutral research. Contrarily, my desire for an increased focus on practice is grounded in an opposite sensibility: In connecting curriculum to material reality, we acknowledge that it cannot be isolated from the world or separated from context and ideology, and that our study of it should therefore be able to explain how, why, and to what ends those connections exist. Such strong grounding in material reality further requires that we also recognize the ways in which those connections manifest through the various lenses of race, class, gender, sexuality, ability, culture, ideology, etc., that our identities embody.

If curriculum studies is to be revitalized through an increased focus on practice, then let us focus on practice as it exists in the context of the complex social, political, and cultural relations of the material world. Such a revitalization would necessarily draw upon aspects of subjectivity found amongst critical curriculum scholars, as well as the attention to practice similar to that for which Wraga and Hlebowitsh call. This revitalization, however, would have to do so on different conceptual grounds that combine the strengths of both, while ameliorating their respective epistemological weaknesses of disconnection from material reality (postmodernist/subjectivity) and false pretenses to objectivity and non-ideology (positivist/pragmatism). Indeed, one of the purposes of *Critical Curriculum Studies* is to aid in such a revitalization.

Critical Curriculum Studies

So far in this introductory chapter, I have grounded *Critical Curriculum Studies* in a fundamental debate within the curriculum field, as well as offered some justifications and discussed the overall sensibilities of this book. As for defining the central terms of this book, namely, "critical," "curriculum," and "consciousness," I would simply assure the reader that I address those difficult terms in subsequent chapters. In Chapter 2, "With and Within the World," drawing on the work critical theorists and researchers such as Freire (1974), Vygotsky (1987), Allman (2007), Marx and Engels (1978), Lukacs (1971), Hartsock (1998a), and others, I outline the epistemological foundations used in my analysis and conceptualization of curriculum. There I essentially argue for what I am calling a dialectical conception of consciousness, one that is philosophically materialist, and one that embraces the dynamic and subjective interplay between humans and the world around them. This conception of consciousness produces two main implications. First, as I take up in Chapter 3, "Epistemology and Educational Experience," it implicates how we conceive of the curriculum generally. Thus, in Chapter 3 I survey some of the conceptions of definitions of "curriculum" (yet another long-standing debate and conversation within the field of curriculum studies), and then, using the works of Huebner (1970), Bernstein (1996), and Vygotsky (1987), and as a direct extension of a dialectical conception of consciousness, I articulate a conception of curriculum as the accessibility of knowledge structured into educational environments.

Second, a dialectical conception of consciousness also points to the social basis of epistemology and knowledge. Thus in Chapter 4, "Developing Curricular Standpoint," making use of the work of Lukacs (1971), Hartsock (1998a), and Harding (2004b), I apply standpoint theory to curriculum studies as a way to explicitly recognize the power relations that are embedded in both the curriculum *and* the study of curriculum. Two central impulses underlie my application of standpoint theory. From a scholarly perspective, it is one of my intentions for this application to act as an intervention within (and possible resolution of) the ongoing pragmatic/positivist and postmodern/subjectivist tensions in curriculum studies, discussed above. From a political perspective, it is also my intention to provide a stronger and more clearly articulated theoretical justification for curriculum work in teaching for social justice.

It follows, then, that in Chapter 5, "Curriculum of the Oppressed," I offer several concrete historical and contemporary examples of curricular standpoint in an attempt to illustrate curricular standpoint in practice *and* as a tool for inquiry in curriculum studies. Finally, in the conclusion I summarize the arguments of this book and consider issues of relative autonomy and the relationship between critical consciousness and the curriculum.

Why Critical Curriculum Studies?

Writing *Critical Curriculum Studies* has felt theoretically and politically ambitious for me. First and foremost, the issues of epistemology and consciousness and how they relate to the politics of knowledge and the curriculum have always been foundational to my own political analysis. So to attempt to articulate these very core concepts in writing and with the intent of sharing my thinking and analyses through this book has been difficult but fruitful for my own development. Additionally, epistemology, consciousness, critical theory, and curriculum are all highly contested concepts in social theory generally, and in education specifically. In this sense, writing this book has meant entering into the fray of some very important yet politically volatile conversations and activist scholarship, while also opening myself up to considerable critique and possible attack by conservatives and other Leftists/ progressives alike.

Writing this book has also felt ambitious for me because, for the most part, *Critical Curriculum Studies* is as largely about theory construction. Like so many other critical scholars and activists, in the past I have mainly engaged in sustained critique in previous work. For instance, much of my book about high-stakes, standardized testing, *Unequal by Design* (Au, 2009f), focused on interrogating the ways that such tests reproduce social and economic inequalities. That critique was historical, political, economic, cultural, empirical, pedagogic, and curricular. And, while I did do some theory building in the final chapters of *Unequal by Design*, much of it was explanatory of the processes that I saw operating through high-stakes testing. To be sure, I want to emphasize that such critique is absolutely necessary: Figuring out what is "wrong" is a necessarily productive and useful way for thinking about what might be "right." Further, given the political, cultural, environmental, and economic stakes of the struggles against rising conservatism, inequality, and neoliberalism that are happening in the United States and around the world (peoples lives are literally at stake), it is a radical imperative that we use critique to expose the inequalities that constitute our material existence (an idea that lies at the heart of both standpoint theory and curricular standpoint discussed in this book). But we also need to build theory. We need to better understand what it is we do in our work, particularly when such work connects education (and other forms of action) to issues of social, political, cultural, and economic justice. Among other objectives, I wanted critical theoretical construction and explanation to be prominent in *Critical Curriculum Studies*.

In addition to building theory, and despite some of the overly-academic hand wringing about the state of the field (mine included), I still believe curriculum studies is important and necessary. Beyer and Liston (1996) provide three compelling justifications for why it is important to analyze the curriculum, particularly within the context of contemporary educational debates. First they note that the curriculum is "the centerpiece of educational activity" that in "its manifest and latent versions ... represents the essence of what education is for" (p. xv). Second, they add that "struggles over the shape of the curriculum are often protracted and heated precisely because they relate to competing visions of ... what sort of future we may have" (p. xv). Third, they observe that the curriculum field is connected to all other aspects of educational inquiry, as well as disciplines outside of education, in terms of both content and form. Thus, studies of the curriculum are of central importance to any discussion within the field of education, particularly if we are to understand both the classroom and social functions that the curriculum fulfills and the implications that extend from those functions (Apple & Beyer, 1988).

Critical Curriculum Studies is thus written in the spirit of Beyer and Liston's (1996) above justifications. I would also add to their list the idea that what we know and learn about the world has a profound impact on how we both view and act within the world. And I use "learning" here in the most general sense, for not only do we experience the curriculum of our schools and systems of education, but, broadly speaking, we also experience the curriculum of our lives. This lived curriculum interplays with our school curriculum, and the whole of it comes together to form our consciousness of the world (consciousness which, admittedly, is always partial and evolving, as well as at times messy and contradictory). So this is why, to me, critical studies of curriculum are important: While the above arguments in the field of curriculum studies are mainly academic conversations amongst theorists, and K-12 teachers and community educators rarely, if ever, take part, curriculum itself is far from just being an academic issue. No matter whether it is in schools or in our lives more generally, curriculum has a relationship to how we think about and understand the world. It enters into our lives and becomes integrated as a part of the total of our experiences. Consequently curriculum also plays an important role in how we make decisions to act (or not to act) in that same world. Put differently, curriculum influences our consciousness as well as how we carry that consciousness forward through praxis (Au, 2007a; Freire, 1974), whether such praxis takes critical or conservative forms (Allman, 2007). This relationship, that between curriculum and the forms of consciousness we develop, is another central reason I undertook the analysis done in this book.

The Author's Social Location(s)

Before continuing, if I'm going to be internally consistent with the politics of my own analysis, I think it is important that the reader understands my own social location(s) and some of my biography, as these shape my own consciousness and undoubtedly contribute to whatever strengths and weaknesses reside in this book. Without thinking too stagnantly about such things, and completely recognizing the fluidity and socially defined nature of whatever categories society uses to identify us (and we admittedly and hesitantly use to define ourselves), in terms of my social location(s) I am currently: heterosexual, of a formerly working class identified family with middle class cultural capital, a mixed blood-hapa haole-Chinese American and White, "able"-bodied, male. Granted, the categories might change, the context might change, or I might change, but this is how I currently identify myself as of this writing.

In terms of the bricolage of my biography: I've got deep roots in the Chinese petit-bourgeoisie of the colonized kingdom/state of Hawai'i (or for those that understand what I mean, I'm 5th generation Chinese American through my paternal grandmother, my Chinese family first coming to Hawai'i in the 1880s). I've also got equally deep roots amongst some of the earliest White settlers/colonizers in New England (I'm supposedly related to a naval officer who came over on the second or third ship after the *Mayflower*). My childhood years came during the nuclear tide of the Reagan Era. I attended extremely diverse, urban elementary schools in West Seattle, and then was one of less than five non-Whites in predominantly White, suburban elementary and middle schools in a Connecticut suburb. I attended a predominantly African American High School and struggled through my identity in my undergraduate education. I was an "honors" student in high school, and I consciously decided to start attending "regular" classes instead. I've been a jock and played collegiate level men's volleyball. I've practiced martial arts and taken hundreds of classes of Bikram Yoga. Both my parents have advanced degrees, while both of my highly intelligent siblings gave up on systems of education that I now know gave up on them as well. I'm also an old school hip hop head and former club DJ (with the turntables and records to prove it), raised on the likes of Public Enemy, Boogie Down Productions, De La Soul, A Tribe Called Quest, Run DMC, The Jungle Brothers, and Queen Latifah, among thousands of others. I've been a credentialed high school teacher and an uncredentialed school administrator. I've taught "honors" students. I've taught "drop-outs." I've taught U.S history, world history, Asian American history, ethnic studies, African studies, American government, eco-literacy, world literature, Asian American literature, and language arts. I've taught urban kids of pretty much all stripes and economic backgrounds. I've worked with really poor rural Whites and even poorer, reservation-based Native American kids. I'm an editor at *Rethinking Schools*. I've been an education activist and organizer. I spent time in Madison, Wisconsin, working on my Ph.D. in curriculum and instruction. I've been a professor in the economically crumbling State of California (in Orange

County, specifically), and am now a professor in the State of Washington. I hail from multiple generations of radical leftists. I try to live my politics, and my friends and family reflect the diversity of the world. I'm a loving father and partner/husband. My wife has taught me to better understand composition and rhetoric and politics and patriarchy and poetry and art and identity and language and culture and food and health and myself and commitment and love. Most of the same could be said of my son.

All these things, and an infinite number more, define who I am and constitute my educative experiences in this world. They have created blind spots and opportunities for illumination alike, all of which contribute to anything I've done—including the writing of this book.

2

WITH AND WITHIN THE WORLD: DEVELOPING A DIALECTICAL CONCEPTION OF CONSCIOUSNESS

Only when we understand the "dialecticity" between consciousness and the world—that is, when we know that we don't have a consciousness here and the world there but, on the contrary, when both of them, the objectivity and the subjectivity, are incarnating dialectically, is it possible to understand what conscientização *is, and to understand the role of consciousness in the liberation of humanity.*

(Freire in Davis & Freire, 1981, p. 62)

Introduction

There is a long history in critical education theory of trying to understand the relationship between schooling, capitalist society, and student consciousness (Au, 2006; Au & Apple, 2009b). Working from a more vulgar, non-dialectical, and deterministic interpretations of Marx and Marxism (often referred to as "orthodox" Marxism), different impulses within this strand of critical educational analysis, for instance, have at times asserted that human consciousness mechanically corresponds to capitalist socio-economic relations, leaving little room for resistance within the contexts of society, culture, and education (see, e.g., Bowles & Gintis, 1976). Other, more fluid and dynamic formulations of the interaction between education and capitalist socio-economic relations have not only theorized the role of conscious human action and subjective agency in the learning process (see, e.g., Apple, 1995, 2004), but also pressed for an understanding of the ways in which humans seek to transform the world around them, with education playing a key role in setting the stage for such transformation to take place (see, e.g., Freire, 1974; Shor & Freire, 1987).

While in other works I have addressed the critically important relationship between schools and capitalist production including what I deem many mis-readings and mis-interpretations of Marxist theory, (see, e.g., Au, 2006, 2007a, 2008b, 2008c, 2010b), this chapter represents something qualitatively different. Here I outline a clearly and relatively concise conception of consciousness—a task I have not had the time or space to undertake in previous work. At first glance, a conception of consciousness may seem out of place in a book about curriculum studies. However, curriculum is fundamentally about learning, about how we see and understand the world. So to me, a thorough and serious treatment of understanding curriculum also requires some attention to how we understand "consciousness," and in this case, "critical consciousness" specifically. In this way, consciousness is central to any discussion of curriculum, and this chapter serves as the foundation for the chapters to follow. Indeed, the conceptual work done here provides the basis for not only how I define "curriculum" in Chapter 3, but also my analysis of the politics and processes that underlay school knowledge generally—a position that has some implications for the field of curriculum theory in that it suggests that consciousness, in some form, lies at the heart of all aspects of the curriculum, no matter how we define it.

Before continuing, I also want to explicitly recognize that this chapter is highly theoretical and conceptual. Should this chapter stand alone on its own, with no actual examples and concrete discussion to follow, the theoretical and conceptual emphasis taken here would be considered problematic by most standards, and rightfully so. However, I do think theory is important because ultimately it is an extension of our practice. How we sum up, analyze, make sense, and generally think about things is important. As such I believe that theory that pushes our conceptions, whether earth-shatteringly profound or merely representing a new spin on something we've taken for granted, is worthwhile. It can help us understand things better, clearer, and in different ways. While I don't purport the work done here to be the end-all, be-all of curriculum studies, I do think, as I argued in Chapter 1, that there is a significant conceptual lag in the field, one that is politically important to address, and one that has implications for education more generally. That said, theory that does not also embrace material reality and concrete practice is, as I also argued in Chapter 1, unmoored, adrift, and potentially lost in the morass of epistemological relativism. Indeed, this chapter and the conception of consciousness I outline here both rest on the idea that theory and practice are intimately and dialectically linked: They only exist relative to each other. Each needs the other in order to exist. They are never alone. There is only the meeting of the two in praxis.

Broadly speaking, my analysis here begins with discussion of what I am calling a dialectical conception of consciousness, which fundamentally frames out how we are simultaneously with and within the world. From there I move onto a brief explanation of philosophical materialism, which connects to how we understand the meeting of theory and action in praxis. This is followed with a discussion of consciousness and how, following activity theory (Vygotsky, 1987), we make use of conceptual tools, which in turn points to the ways that consciousness is social in nature. I then address some conceptions of consciousness and attempt to pull the analysis together into an understanding of how we might conceive of critical consciousness, one that takes into account theories of relative autonomy and the social construction of consciousness as part of understanding the relationship between individual, conscious transformation and social transformation. This particular discussion further highlights the relative collectivity from within which we all "think," and thus cuts against much of the mainstream gravitation towards thinking as a product of autonomous individuality. Finally, I conclude this chapter with some implications that a dialectical conception of consciousness has for curriculum studies.

The Dialectics of Consciousness

While dialectics constitutes its own philosophical subfield with its own treatises and explications on dialectical logic, for the purposes of this discussion, I mainly focus on some basic principles of how dialectics applies to our conscious understanding of the world. In short, at the heart of dialectics is the idea that all "things" are actually processes, that these processes are in constant motion, or development, and that this development is driven by the tension created by two interrelated and internally related opposites acting in contradiction with each other (Allman, 2007; Gadotti, 1996; Ollman, 2003; Woods & Grant, 2002). These two opposites require each other to exist, for together they make up a unified whole (Allman, 1999). Hence, unlike the positivist logics associated with Enlightenment rationality—which focuses on isolation of individual pieces or phenomenon as well as simple, linear, mechanical cause-and-effect relationships (Benton & Craib, 2001), dialectical relationships are actually deeply and intimately integrated with each other in fluid and dynamic movement together. As Hartsock (1998a) explains,

> The dialectical mode of understanding provides a means for us to investigate the manifold ways social forces are related, a way to examine a world in which "objects" are defined by the relations coming to focus in them, and in which these objects are constantly changing in response to the changing weights of other factors.
>
> *(p. 93)*

Thus, a dialectical conception sees the world as a multilayered, interrelated system, a living totality, a dynamic chain of relationships and processes (Gadotti, 1996; Ollman, 2003; Sayers, 1990).

In a dialectical conception of consciousness, then, as Freire (1998) asserts, "Consciousness and the world cannot be understood separately, in a dichotomized fashion, but rather must be seen in their contradictory relations" (p. 19). Dialectically speaking, such "contradictory relations" mean that we have to envision human consciousness coming from an interrelated, non-dichotomized relationship *with* and *within* the material world, including the human capacity to act back upon that very same world. In this way consciousness must be understood as a process where the dialectical interaction between humans and their environments continually unfolds and develops, where "being" (ontology) in the world and our theory of knowledge (epistemology) of that world are dynamically connected (Allman, 1999) as we simultaneously react to and act upon the world in which we live (Au, 2007a).

Materialism and Consciousness

Fundamentally, a dialectical conception of consciousness is rooted in the idea that human understanding and knowledge of the world originates, develops, and grows from human interaction with the material world around (Allman, 1999, 2007; Engels, 1940; Vygotsky, 1987)—a material world of which they themselves are a part, and one that is also constituted by culture and society. As Allman (1999) explains:

> [I]deas and concepts arise from the relations between people and from relations between people and their material world (the world created by human beings as well as the natural world) ... [where] we actively and sensuously experience these relations; therefore, our consciousness is actively produced within our experience of our social, material and natural existence.
>
> *(p. 37)*

This provides the basis for materialism in a dialectical conception of consciousness.

Materialism, in a philosophical sense, is the idea that matter precedes consciousness, that the material world has existed and would exist regardless of whether or not any humans or divine beings conceived of such existence (Marx & Engels, 1978). Relative to how we understand epistemology, how we "know" what we "know," a materialist conception is important because it recognizes that our consciousness of the world is in a sense fundamentally produced by the world itself, and not the other way around. Further, a materialist conception also recognizes that, as Hartsock (1998a) explains,

> Not only are human powers affirmed and realized through the objective world, but the objective world becomes an extension of ourselves in both human and nonhuman forms. All objects come to be objects *for us*, with real relations to human needs, hopes, and possibilities.
>
> *(p. 95, original emphasis)*

As Hartsock suggests, materialism is thus implicated in a dialectical conception of consciousness in that the world that we interact with and within is also an extension of human relations. This connection between philosophical materialism and the dialectical conception of consciousness is critically important because it actively acknowledges the centrality of human action to transform the world, praxis.

It is critical to note here that, just because consciousness, as Allman (1999) suggests above, "is actively produced within our experience of our social, material and cultural existence" (p. 37), does not mean that consciousness is totally determined by external material factors, nor does it mean that humans do not have the capability to determine how they think about and "know" the world around them. Rather, just as the relative autonomy of schools from economic relations must be understood in non-deterministic, non-mechanical ways (Au, 2006), the relationship between consciousness and our material environments must also be conceived of in the same way: *dialectically*. There exists interaction, unity, and dynamic fluidity in the connected interchange between humans and their social, cultural, and material environments. Indeed, as I take up in more detail in the conclusion, it is the relative autonomy of both schools and consciousness that creates the space for the curriculum to take up a more critical stance and act as a conceptual tool in the praxis of working for social justice (Hursh & Ross, 2000).

Praxis

The dialectical nature of this conception of consciousness thus leads to several important implications. The first is that consciousness is directly linked with action. Essentially, this implication is the extension of the dialectical link between "being" (ontology) and "knowing" (epistemology), discussed above. Because we are in constant, dialectical interaction with the material world (a world that is also socio-cultural since it also contains human relations), we come to know things vis-à-vis our inseparable relationships with the totality of our environments. Thus, our very existence means we "are not only *in* the world, but *with* the world" (Freire, 1982a, p. 3, original emphasis) at all times. However, to be *with* the world, to exist in this inseparable relationship, to be always interacting with our environment, is a process that requires constant activity, constant interchange, and constant reflection. Put more simply, "being" is in fact an activity, and in a dialectical conception of consciousness, that activity is being *in* and *with* the world.

This process of constant, simultaneous thinking and being in and with the world is called "praxis." Freire (1982c) explains that:

> [H]uman beings ... are beings of "praxis": of action and of reflection. Humans find themselves marked by the results of their own actions in their relations with the world, and through the action on it. By acting they transform; by transforming they create a reality which conditions their manner of acting.
>
> *(p. 102)*

Here Freire is trying to get at the dialectical link between reflection and action. While praxis is often defined as the application of theory to practice and is often illustrated as a step-by-step, linear process, praxis is more correctly conceived dialectically as the "inseparable unity of thought and practice" (Allman, 2007, p. 33). Indeed, we might even consider human *being* as the continuous, simultaneous and connected processes of *thinking* (reflection) and *doing* (action).

Consciousness and Tools

Thinking and doing (reflecting and acting relative to our environments) are themselves activities. They are all part of the human praxis within a dialectical conception of consciousness. Human activity, however, does not happen in the abstract. Rather, as another aspect of a dialectical conception of consciousness, it is important to understand that humans make use of physical and conceptual tools in their interactions with the social, cultural, and material environment. In the Marxist tradition this was first conceived by Engels (1940), who originally discussed the role that physical tools (e.g., farming tools and even hands-as-tools) played in human activity and development as they interacted with their physical environments (simultaneously shaping and being shaped by these environments). Granted, while there certainly are critiques to be made of parts of Engels' analysis, this particular formulation has proved fruitful in research in the relationship between human activity and learning (see, e.g., Bakhurst, 1997; Cole & Engeström, 1997; Engeström, 1989, 1999; Scribner, 1997; Zinchenko, 1996).

Vygotsky (1987), in his work in child development and learning, extended Engels' (1940) materialist conception of the human-environment dialectical inter-action vis-à-vis physical tools to include the use of conceptual and cultural tools such as sign systems/language as a mediating factor in human development and learning (Cole & Scribner, 1978). In his research Vygotsky (1987) essentially found that we use the cultural/conceptual tools of signs and sign systems (i.e. language) not only for social activity, but also to make sense of our experiences with the physical and social worlds and develop our capacity to think. Although he does not explicitly frame it as such, Freire (1974, 1992) also arrives at the same conclusion, where he sees how literacy, as a conceptual tool, can be used to critically reflect on social conditions as part of a process that fosters the development of certain forms of consciousness amongst students (Au, 2009c). Hartsock (1998a) puts it thusly:

> Although human beings do not create the world from nothing, human activity does produce existence differentiated into individuals, species, and all categories we take as given—categories and concepts that respond to specific problems posed for us by social life. At the same time, however, consciousness itself is a social product. Human consciousness and the shape of human society depend on each other. What can be appropriated (constructively incorporated into human consciousness) varies with the practical forms of human activity.
>
> *(p. 88)*

This relationship between praxis and the tools humans use to dialectically interact with their social and physical worlds connects directly to another aspect of a dialectical conception of consciousness: that consciousness is fundamentally social in origin and structure (Marx & Engels, 1978).

Social Consciousness

> To paraphrase a well-known position of Marx's, we could say that humans' psychological nature represents the aggregate of internalized social relations that have become functions for the individual and forms of his/her structure.
>
> *(Vygotsky, 1981, p. 164)*

Freire (1987, 1995) explains the social nature of consciousness where, through his literacy work, he concludes that because humans are part of the world, and that because our consciousness comes from dialectical interaction with that world, other humans included, ultimately consciousness shapes and is shaped by both our physical and social worlds (Roberts, 2003). Thus, because we use language and communication in this relationship, for Freire (1982c) "Subjects cannot think alone" and there "is no longer an 'I think' but 'we think'" (p. 137). In this sense, "individuality must be understood as a social phenomenon … " because "human existence in all its forms must be seen as the product of human activity" (Hartsock, 1998a, p. 47). Or, as Gramsci (1971) puts it, "Our capacity to think and act on the world is dependent on other people who are themselves also both subjects and objects of history" (p. 346), such that we cannot conceive of consciousness without taking it to be fundamentally social.

This point, that within a dialectical conception of consciousness our thinking is essentially and fundamentally social in origin, was made by Vygotsky (1929, 1981, 1987) in several different settings and studies. For instance, Vygotsky (1981) discusses the role of signs (language) as mediating tools in the cultural development of children:

> If it is correct that the sign initially is a means of social interaction and only later becomes a means of behavior for the individual, it is quite clear that the cultural development is based on the use of signs and their inclusion in a general system of behavior that initially was external and social. In general, we could say that the relations among higher mental functions were at some earlier time actual relations among people.
>
> *(p. 158)*

Thus, Vygotsky concludes, because we use socially constructed language systems to mediate our interactions with our social and physical contexts, ultimately our consciousness originates socially (Bakhurst, 1991).

Indeed, the dialectical conception of consciousness leads us to understand how the social nature of consciousness can be seen in our reliance upon language and sign systems for thinking and communication of ideas, as Vygotsky (1981) points to above. The basic logic is this: All linguistic meaning is drawn from socio-linguistic, cultural, and discursive contexts. Put slightly differently, we cannot make meaning of words unless we have a systematic, social, historical, and cultural context in which to make linguistic and conceptual sense of them in the first place (Gee,

2008). Logically, we might argue that we would have no need to develop linguistic systems (which, fundamentally are systems of ideas) unless we needed to communicate with someone beyond our individual selves. There is no need to capture thought in a linguistic (or symbolic) system unless we intend to share it beyond our immediate consciousness. Hence, because our linguistic systems function as tools for human interaction with each other and their material environments, they carry social relations in their very structure and meaning (Bernstein, 1996; Volosinov, 1986). In a most basic sense then, our consciousness is less individually based and more a product of human interaction and relations.

Further, as Leont'ev (1981) discusses, the social nature of consciousness runs beyond just our use of language, because, as he explains:

> Consciousness is not given from the beginning and is not produced by nature: consciousness is a product of society: it is *produced* ... Thus the process of internalization is not the *transferal* of an external activity to a pre-existing, internal "plane of consciousness": it is the process in which this internal plane is *formed*.
>
> *(pp. 56–57, original emphasis)*

Leont'ev's point is particularly important because he reminds us that, in a dialectical conception of consciousness, consciousness does not just appear. Rather, if we are to understand consciousness in a materialist manner, we have to recognize that it is produced by the meanings humans develop vis-à-vis social and cultural interaction. Further still, as Leont'ev argues, the internal structure of our consciousness is itself formed by social production—which requires that we consider the possibility that the social basis of our consciousness runs so deep as to be embedded in how consciousness is structured and organized. Indeed, this point lies at the center of Bernstein's (1977, 1990, 1996) work, who argues that the very categories we use and in which we operate in educational discourse contain power relations within the categories themselves—a formulation that has proven correct in my own research (see, e.g., Au, 2008c; 2009f) as well as that of others (see, e.g., Sleeter & Stillman, 2005; Wong & Apple, 2003).

Being Conscious of Our Consciousness

However, for all of the aspects of a dialectical conception of consciousness I have discussed thus far, the question of what consciousness "is" still remains. What is key here, and runs as a strand among and within all of the above discussion, is the process of reflection (meant here in the sense of "consideration" or "thinking"). Our dialectical interactions with our environment are, in part, guided by our continual reflection and subsequent responses/activities based on that same reflection. This is human ontology, the defining praxis of our being. Indeed, as Hartsock (1998a) explains, this amalgam of reflection, activity, and the social nature of how we know and understand the world, leads directly to how we might also understand consciousness more specifically:

> Social knowledge, then, is best understood as a kind of self-awareness. ... First, persons are active and involved in forming or creating a conceptualized and meaningful world. Without involvement there can be no reality for us. Second, human beings are a part of the subject matter as knowing individuals—the subject of all specifically human knowledge. Moreover, through the appropriation, the incorporation, or experience ... we make both the natural and the social world a part of our humanness.
>
> *(p. 99)*

Thus, fundamentally, "consciousness" requires active consideration of how one interacts with one's social, cultural, and material environment, or in Hartsock's above words, "make both the natural and social world a part of our humanness." In this sense we might say that, "*Consciousness is intentionality towards the world*" (Freire in Davis & Freire, 1981, p. 58, original emphasis), where we develop "the capacity to adapt ... to reality *plus* the critical capacity to make choices and transform ... reality" (Freire, 1982a, p. 4, original emphasis).

Dewey (1916) explains this aspect of consciousness in the following way:

> To identify acting with an aim and intelligent activity is enough to show its value—its function in experience ... To be conscious is to be aware of what we are about; conscious signifies the deliberate, observant, planning traits of activity. Consciousness is nothing which we have which gazes idly on the scene around one or which has impressions made upon it by physical things; it is a name for the purposeful quality of an activity, for the fact that it is directed by an aim. Put the other way about, to have an aim is to act with meaning, not like an automatic machine; it is to *mean* to do something and to perceive the meaning of things in light of that intent.
>
> *(pp. 103–4, original emphasis)*

The last part of Dewey's point here is particularly important, because acting consciously—with intent, also carries with it a reflection on the intent itself, what Dewey says is to "perceive the meaning of things in light of that intent." Thus we might conceive of consciousness as "consciousness *of* consciousness" (Freire, 1974, p. 107, original emphasis), where, in Vygotsky's (1987) words, "Conscious awareness is an act of consciousness whose object is the activity of consciousness itself" (p. 190). In this regard consciousness may be understood as a meta-awareness of the interplay of our thoughts and real-world actions, an awareness that develops through an active process of first decoding reality, only to recode through the envisioning of alternative structures (Au, 2009c; Freire, 1974, 1982b; Shor, 1992).

Thinking about our thinking—being conscious of our consciousness—is thus an extension of the dialectical unity between reflection and action because of its relationship to volition and human activity in the world. If we are conscious about something, then our "doing" is guided by our "thinking," and vice versa. In this regard consciousness allows us to "become consciously aware of [our] context and [our] condition as a human being as Subject ... [and] become an instrument of choice" (Freire, 1982a, p. 56) because we can "reflect critically about [our] conditioning process and go beyond it" (Freire, 1998, p. 20) in our actions.

Critical Consciousness

Despite my use of the above definitions, I want to emphasize that thinking about consciousness in terms of volition, intentionality, and/or meta-awareness is not enough: People can and do think quite "consciously" as they act in oppressive ways in our world on individual and institutional levels. For instance, historically the U.S. government has operated very strategically and with much forethought in its campaigns to undermine democratic movements domestically (Zinn, 1995) and internationally (see, e.g., Steenland, 1974). Similarly, neoliberals and policymakers have acted with intention and conscious awareness as they sought to dismantle New Orleans public schools by breaking the teachers' union, closing schools, and constructing the district along the lines of a free market system that is leading to massive educational inequalities (Buras, 2007; Dingerson, 2008).

Thus, we have to recognize that defining consciousness simply along the lines of active intent and volition falls short within progressive forms of educational theory and practice (Au, 2009c; Fine, 1997), and that a dialectical conception of consciousness necessarily requires an embrace of "criticality" (Allman, 2007; Freire, 1974). Consequently, the "critical" in critical reflection is central because to look at something critically requires that we become aware of our context to see how external relations impinge upon our thinking and acting—our praxis. Furthermore, given the social nature of consciousness, discussed above, critically reflecting on our own consciousness is simultaneously both an individually and socially-cognitive move because it necessitates a critical reflection on the social structures that shape our consciousness—it is both a reflection on our own thinking as well as a critical reflection on the structure of society itself. Subsequently, being critical implies making "supra-empirical connections" (Vygotsky, 1987) in our cognitive and material relationship with the external world, as well as between the relations we see operating within that world. Following Lukacs (1971), then, critical consciousness in this sense also implies understanding how one "fits" into the totality of interconnected relations.

Freire (in Davis & Freire, 1981) explains the relationship between critical reflection and our contexts in terms of education for freedom (as opposed to education for oppression), where he observes:

[E]ducation for freedom implies constantly, permanently, the exercise of consciousness turning in on itself in order to discover itself in the relationships with the world, trying to explain the reasons which can make clear the concrete situation people have in the world.

(p. 59)

In discovering "the relationships with the world" and explaining the "reasons which can make clear the concrete situation people have in the world," through critical reflection we seek to develop more systematic analyses of these relationships—analyses whose point is to understand our world in ways that "exceed the limits of actual and ... potential experience" (Vygotsky, 1987, p. 180). Examining our relationships in a systematic way allows us to see things that we did not necessarily see before in the immediacy of our everyday experiences: We may learn something new about an object we've taken for granted on a day-to-day basis, or we may learn something new about an object that we have never actually physically experienced (Au, 2007c).

Additionally, it is important in the context of the present discussion to recognize that reflection is always both retrospective and introspective. There is no choice but for it to be retrospective since we cannot "reflect" into the future because time continues to move beyond the present moment into the past. Further, because of our individual consciousness, reflection is also introspective because we cannot reflect (nor think) for someone else—even if the social nature of consciousness (and language) requires that we need other humans to systematically think about the world (Freire, 1974). Rather, we can only look within ourselves and consider our relationships with our external environments as we have experienced them as well as ask others to do the same.

Learning and developing critical consciousness thus require retrospection and introspection—looking backwards and inwards to consider how our experiences and the outward social structures shape our consciousness. All of which points to the power of the "critical" moment of reflection, because it is in that moment that we shift our understanding of whatever it is we are considering. This shift in perspective is important because, "To perceive something in a different way means to acquire new potentials for acting with respect to it ... " (Vygotsky, 1987, p. 190)—or "go beyond" our "conditioning process," as Freire (1998, p. 20) suggests above.

A central issue to consider relative to a dialectical conception of consciousness, then, is the politics that guide both our critical reflections and our actions, because these politics help dictate what new potentials for acting manifest in our consciousness. Allman (2007) talks about these politics in terms of "critical/revolutionary praxis" and "reproductive/uncritical praxis." Reproductive praxis, Allman explains, is a form of praxis where people "only engage in the social relations into which they are born, assuming all the while that these relations, or practices, are natural and inevitable" (p. 34). This type of engagement, Allman continues, "will serve only to reproduce the extant relations and conditions" (p. 34). Conversely, in critical praxis people "choose to critically question the existing social relations and to engage in transforming, or abolishing, them whilst also developing new social relations and conditions aimed at creating a better existence for all human beings" (p. 34). It is this critical questioning of inequitable social relations and working towards their abolition, while simultaneously developing new, more equitable relations (including more equitable social, cultural, and material environments), that inhabits a dialectical conception of consciousness and ultimately defines critical consciousness.

Conclusion

In this chapter I have outlined a dialectical conception of consciousness. To summarize, within this conception:

- Consciousness is essentially produced through human interaction with our environment (Allman, 1999; Marx & Engels, 1978);
- Being and knowing are dynamically intertwined within the dialectical relationship between consciousness and our environment (Allman, 1999; Freire, 1998);
- Our consciousness is expressed through praxis—the dialectically unified process of thinking and doing (Allman, 2007; Freire, 1982a, 1982c);
- We use tools to interact with our environment, and such tools are central to the development of consciousness (Vygotsky, 1987);
- Consciousness is fundamentally social in its development and structure (Leont'ev, 1981; Vygotsky, 1987);
- Consciousness implies thinking about thinking, volitional action, and intentionality towards the world, where such intentionality is guided by understanding connections and social relations (Davis & Freire, 1981; Vygotsky, 1987);
- Being critical in our reflection is central to developing consciousness, and such reflection creates the potential to challenge existing, unequal social relations and work towards more equitable and just social change (Allman, 2007; Freire, 1974). This is what defines "critical consciousness"—a term I will focus on using from this point forward in this book;
- There is some level of relative autonomy of both schools and consciousness from the socio-economic structures (Au, 2008c; Bernstein, 1996). This too is a part of our potential to use education and human action to make a more just world.

In outlining a dialectical conception of consciousness, I realize that I am entering into a long, difficult, and controversial subject area. Being "conscious" means a lot of things to a lot of people, including simply meaning being "awake" as opposed to being unconscious or asleep in a physical/biological sense. To be sure, everyone makes their way in the world, thinking and interacting with and upon their environments. In this basic regard one might argue that everyone is "conscious." But I think many of the critical researchers, activists, educators, and practitioners I've relied upon in my discussion here do not see consciousness in only this way. Not everyone actively thinks about their thinking, takes time to consider and mull the wide range of implications and meanings, both immediate and distant, that their actions might carry. And it is the development of this type of thinking that is the focus of my analysis here: I am less interested in arguing about whether or not someone is biologically awake. I am more interested in thinking through what it means to consciously consider how we "are" in the world, how we manifest and embody social processes and social relations, and how we contemplate the effects of our actions and take further actions to rectify mistakes or problems. So, ultimately, how one defines "consciousness" is less important than how we define "critical consciousness," or "critical praxis" in Allman's (2007) terminology, if we are interested in forms of education that prepare students to thoughtfully and constructively engage with their physical and social worlds.

In this chapter, then, I am suggesting that curriculum is fundamentally about consciousness and the forms it can take relative to schooling/education/classroom practice. Indeed, how we conceive of consciousness is fundamental to how we understand the curriculum—hence, this chapter functions as the fulcrum upon which the rest of my analysis rests. In the balance are two key implications that a dialectical conception of consciousness holds for understanding curriculum: How we might define "curriculum" and how we understand the relationship between curriculum and society. Each of these implications will be taken up in Chapters 3 and 4, respectively.

3

EPISTEMOLOGY AND EDUCATIONAL EXPERIENCE: CURRICULUM, THE ACCESSIBILITY OF KNOWLEDGE, AND COMPLEX ENVIRONMENTAL DESIGN

> *The responsibility of the curriculum person, then, is to design and criticize specialized envir-onments which embody the dialectical relationships valued in a given society … These envir-onments must encourage the moment of vision, when the past and future are the horizons of the individual's present so that [their] own potentiality for being is grasped.*
>
> *(Huebner, 1999a, pp. 138–39)*

In Chapter 2 I outlined a dialectical conception of consciousness, a conception that lays at the core of my framework for critical curriculum studies. Here I take on what this conception of consciousness implies for how we understand, conceive, and define "curriculum." I begin with an overview of various definitions of the term "curriculum." This overview will hopefully provide a landscape for the particular definition and conception which I am advocating here. Then, drawing largely on the work of the curricular theorist Dwayne Huebner, I make the case that, based on a dialectical conception of consciousness developed in Chapter 2, curriculum can be defined as a form of complex environmental design. Finally, I further develop Huebner's conception of curriculum by incorporating both Vygotsky's work on using tools for human development and learning, as well as Bernstein's work on the classification and framing of knowledge in pedagogic discourse.

Conceptions and Definitions of Curriculum

When thinking about the meaning of curriculum, it is important to begin by acknowledging that there is no agreement within the field of curriculum studies on a single definition of "curriculum" (Beauchamp, 1982; Jackson, 1980; Kliebard, 1989). Rather, as Jackson (1996) explains, " [A]ll definitions are parts of arguments … All we can do in the final analysis is to proffer reasoned arguments in support of one definition over the other" (p. 12). As such, it is important to understand some of the contours of the struggle over defining the word "curriculum," as doing so helps us understand the particular definition for which I am arguing here.

Historically the actual word "curriculum" has its roots in the Latin word *currere*, which means "to run a course" (Eisner, 1994), and was first used at the University of Glasgow in the 17th century to describe "a formal course of study that the students completed" (Harden, 2001, p. 335). The historical definition, that of a course of study, is perhaps the simplest and easiest for us to see because it is evident in the way so many schools are organized around graduation requirements consisting of a battery of subject matter classes to be passed. Despite its straightforward simplicity, this most basic definition does not allow for the actual complexity of the ways curriculum actually manifests in classrooms and schools. Given this, curricular theorists and scholars have given considerable attention to different, more nuanced ways to think about just what defines the curriculum.

Near the turn of the 20th century, for instance, both Dewey (1902) and Bobbitt (1972 [1918]) advanced a basic definition of curriculum that we could associate with "educational experience." As Jackson (1996) explains, Dewey (1902) viewed the curriculum in a variety of ways (as we will see later in this chapter), including casting it in terms of "continuous reconstruction, moving from the child's present experience out into that represented by the organized bodies of truth that we call studies" (p. 11). Bobbitt (1972 [1918]), working from within a different framework, similarly asserted that:

> The curriculum may, therefore, be defined in two ways: (1) it is the entire range of experiences, both undirected and directed, concerned in unfolding the abilities of the individual; or (2) it is the series of consciously directed training experiences that the schools use for completing and perfecting the unfoldment.
>
> *(p. 43)*

One of the difficulties of defining curriculum-as-experience is that everything counts as experience, so curriculum thus becomes everything. Such a definition is problematic because once we define it as everything the curriculum ceases to exist as a distinct concept and loses any meaning. As Apple (1978) explains,

> [I]f curriculum theory … is to concern itself only with experience, then it becomes identical with everything we do. There can be very little serious ethical, political, or even aesthetic dialog. All things are equal; all values are relative; all possibilities are the same; everything we do is an experience. It is everything so it is nothing identifiable.
>
> *(p. 515)*

Educational scholars have thus critiqued this view for its all encompassing vagueness (Jackson, 1996).

Modern curricular scholars have framed out multiple, sometimes competing and sometimes complimentary ways of defining "curriculum." Eisner (1994), for instance, suggests there are three types of curriculum that all schools teach: 1. The explicit curriculum, which consists of the stated goals and objectives; 2. The implicit curriculum, which he identifies as "the ways in which the culture of both the classroom and the school socializes children to values that are a part of the structure of those places" (p. 88). As examples of the implicit curriculum Eisner includes the values and images displayed by texts, the ways schools "foster compliant behavior" (p. 89), and the way grades are used to teach the value of an "extrinsic reward structure" (p. 90); and 3. The null curriculum, or, what schools do not teach (see also, Flinders, Noddings, & Thornton, 1986).

Interestingly, Eisner (1994) equates the "implicit curriculum" with what is also referred to as the "hidden curriculum," (Apple, 2004) but does so only in passing. In the process Eisner (1994) ultimately glosses the more political aspects of the hidden curriculum, aspects that might differentiate it from that of the implicit curriculum (however slight such differentiation may or may not be). While there is a long history and literature devoted to discussion of what has been called the hidden curriculum (for an excellent review of this literature, see, Margolis, Soldatenko, Acker, & Gair, 2001), the concept of the hidden curriculum is attached to social relations in that it refers to "the tacit teaching of social and economic norms and expectations to students in schools … " (Apple, 2004, p. 42), where these "norms and values … are related to working in this unequal society" (Apple, 1995, p. 87). Or, as Anyon (1980) explains with regards to her research:

> The "hidden curriculum" of school work is tacit preparation for relating to the process of production in a particular way. Differing curricular, pedagogical, and pupil evaluation practices emphasize different cognitive and behavioral skills in each social setting and thus contribute to the development in children certain potential relationships to physical and symbolic capital, to authority, and to the process of work … These differences may not only contribute to the development in the children in each social class of certain types of economically significant relationships and not others, but would thereby help to *reproduce* this system of relations in society. In the contribution to the reproduction of unequal social relations lies a theoretical meaning, and social consequence, of classroom practice.
>
> *(pp. 89–90, original emphasis)*

The "enacted curriculum" is yet another conception of curriculum, one that synthesizes and expands upon other curricular theorists' analyses. Drawing on the work of Jackson (1968), Dreeben (1968), and others (Wallat & Green, 1979), Weisz (1989), for instance, defines the "enacted curriculum" as consisting of the combination of the "overt curriculum" (that which is specifically planned for—which roughly equates to Eisner's explicit curriculum), the "hidden curriculum," and what

Weisz refers to as the "social curriculum," which consists of the social interactions that take place in the classroom. Weisz's research goes on to identify two additional types of curriculum in her study. These include the "masked curriculum," which conveys "academic content while 'masquerading' as procedural/management or informal activity" (p. 158)—such as embedding a math exercise within the counting of lunch money, and the "unofficial curriculum" which refers to "a spontaneous (unintended) lesson, or activity, that a teacher has students engage in that is not included in the official policy document or even in the lesson plan" (pp. 158–59). In this regard Weisz's conception of the "enacted curriculum" essentially consists of five distinct aspects of curriculum grouped as a constellation to describe classroom activity.

Quite differently from other scholars, Kliebard (1989) offers a definition of curriculum by way of the problems and issues that confront curriculum as a field of study. For him, the curriculum is thus what is taught (with implicit or explicit justification), who it is taught to (including the conditions of the audience to which it is being taught), how it is taught (pedagogy), and the bringing together of knowledge into an integrated whole. I have advocated a definition of curriculum akin to Kliebard's above definition in previous work of my own (Au, 2007b, 2009f). There I have argued that when we discuss curriculum (particularly relative to high-stakes, standardized testing), not only do we have to include content knowledge, we also have to recognize that what we teach directly implicates how we teach (pedagogy), as well as the form or structure we give to that knowledge as it is communicated.

Greene (1971) characterizes the curriculum as signifying the "possibility for [the learner] as an existing person" to make "sense of [their] own life-world ... " and promising "occasions for ordering the materials of that world, for imposing 'configurations' by means of experiences and perspectives made available for personally conducted cognitive action" (p. 253). Greene's definition revolves around sense-making, and it does so in terms of possibility and promise. For Greene, curriculum has a purpose, to enable the student to "recognize that reason and order may represent the culminating step in [their] constitution of a world ... [that they] may realize what it is to generate the structures of discipline on [their] own initiative ... Curriculum can offer the possibility for students to be the makers of such networks ... " (p. 268).

Such a variety of definitions and conceptions of curriculum can, arguably, be confusing, seemingly over academic, and unnecessarily complicated. We could certainly argue that they contribute to the crisis in curriculum studies I discussed in Chapter 1. I am in agreement with Jackson (1996), however, when he states that, "A function [curriculum definitions] clearly serves to provide a language for helping us to think and talk about the variety of curricular issues that might otherwise be overlooked" (p. 12). So in this sense, we might say that the point of having so many different definitions and conceptions of curriculum is the point of curriculum studies itself: It is all part of a general attempt to see and think about and interrogate aspects of the curriculum that others may have missed, or at the very least understand curriculum in a new light.

However, while there is some value in understanding curriculum differently and seeing it in new ways, I find that many earlier conceptions leave me wanting. The kind of conception I want to develop has to not only address identity and the subjectivity of experience, but also material reality in such a way as to highlight critical resistance to, and transformation of, dominant social, political, and economic relations. Additionally, the kind of conception of curriculum I feel is necessary has to relate to the classroom practices of teachers, but also has to have enough theoretical explanatory power to interrogate the complex material and social relations embodied by those very same practices. I also think that we need a conception of curriculum that is not reified, one that sees curriculum mainly as relations and processes and thus cannot be mistaken for being structural-functionalist in regards to knowledge and consciousness. At the same time, I want such a conception of curriculum to also recognize that both knowledge and consciousness are very much structured by relations of power. Further, the conception of curriculum I am after must explicitly recognize that learning and consciousness are connected, and as such, our understanding of the world is simultaneously both clouded and illuminated by our identities as well as the social locations that produced those same identities. And I am not convinced earlier conceptions of curriculum can perform the difficult task of meeting all of the above criteria. Thus, in what follows I outline a conception of curriculum as a problem of complex environmental design that attempts to selectively make different knowledge available to different students as part of a broader process of shaping student consciousness—in either hegemonic or critical, reproductive or revolutionary (using the terms of Allman, 2007), conservative or progressive ways. It is my intent for this conception of curriculum to provide the complexity, criticality, attention to practice, recognition of subjectivity, and structural considerations discussed above.

The Curriculum as a Problem of Complex Environmental Design

Dewey was one of the earliest advocates of viewing education and the curriculum environmentally. In "The Situation as Regards the Course of Study" (Dewey, 1901), he observes that the actual structures of the school ultimately regulate educative interactions:

> It is easy to fall into the habit of regarding the mechanics of school organization and administration as something comparatively external and indifferent to educational purposes and ideals. We think of the grouping of children in classes, the arrangement of grades, the machinery by which the course of study is made out and laid down, the method by which it is carried into effect, the system of selecting teachers and of assigning them to their work, of paying and promoting them, as, in a way, matters of mere practical convenience and expediency. We forget that it is precisely such things as these that really control the whole system, even on its distinctively educational side.

> No matter what is the accepted precept and theory, no matter what the legislation of the school board or the mandate of the school superintendent, the reality of education is found in the personal and face-to-face contact of teacher and child. The conditions that underlie and regulate this contact dominate the educational situation.
>
> *(pp. 337–38)*

While in this case he does not use the term "environment," we can already see Dewey's acknowledgment that the learning process itself is indeed structured by the conditions external to the "reality of education ... found in the personal and face-to-face contact of teacher and child." However, Dewey is even more explicit about the role that classroom environment plays in education in his *Democracy and Education* (Dewey, 1916), where he asserts that, "We never educate directly, but indirectly by means of the environment. Whether we permit chance environments to do the work, or whether we design environments for the purpose makes a great difference" (p. 19). For Dewey, the environment "consists of those conditions that promote or hinder, stimulate or inhibit, the *characteristic* activities of a living being" (p. 11, original emphasis), and is "the only way in which adults consciously control the kind of education which the immature get by controlling the environment in which they act, and hence think and feel" (pp. 18–19). In this way, one might envision the environment as the "intermediary of influence" of the student (Hanson, 2002). Consequently, Dewey was a fairly strict pragmatist and empiricist (Shook, 2000), and as such his thinking exhibited certain aspects of behavioralism, individualism, and subjective idealism associated with the psychology of that time (Gonzalez, 1982; Smith, 1985).

Scholarly discussions about the importance of the "learning environment" are ongoing, where educational researchers are studying, for instance, the role that furniture (physical environment) plays in education (Cornell, 2002), system designs for literacy development (Brown & Campione, 1996), the creation of "powerful learning environments" that aim at developing higher order thinking skills (van Merrienboer & Paas, 2003), or the discourse ecologies that shape writing (Dobrin & Weisser, 2002). While these scholars are indeed addressing the issue of learning environments, they do not explicitly entertain discussions of the theoretical relationship between the curriculum and the classroom/learning environment per se. Aside from a few notable instances (e.g., Harden, 2001), specific theorizing about the curriculum as environmental design has seemed to wane over the years.

There are some conceptions of learning in relation to the environment—and the curriculum's role in that learning—that are less focused on the individual and less interested in linear accounts of experience. These conceptions of curriculum as a problem of complex environmental design posit a dialectical relationship between the learner and the environment—as discussed in the previous chapter, as well as a dialectical conception of this relationship over time (past, present, and future). The curricular theorist Dwayne Huebner (1970, 1999a) offers perhaps the most complex explanation of this conception, and it is his conception that I would like to offer as a powerful and socially and politically relevant way to understand the curriculum. Huebner was an educational philosopher, and he addressed his conception of the curriculum as complex environmental design over the course of several papers and from several different angles. What follows is a summary and synthesis of Huebner's conception as it spans across several of his essays.

Dwayne Huebner and the Design of Educational Environments

> [O]ne of the tasks of the curricular theorist is to focus [their] attention on the characteristics of the educative environment. This involves primarily development of a descriptive language that will enable [they] and other curricularists to catalog and chart the environmental dimensions of practice. It might be said ... that the curricularists' responsibility is to fabricate an environment that educates.
>
> *(Huebner, 1999b, p. 222)*

In his essay, "The Tasks of the Curricular Theorist," Huebner (1999b) outlines three aspects of the educative environment. The first is physical materials; as Huebner notes, "the curriculum consists partly of the buildup of capital investment in the educative material ... " (p. 221). This includes books, media, furniture, equipment, and even the architectural structure of the buildings. The second aspect is the "language and symbol systems used for discourse among students and teachers within that environment" (p. 221). For Huebner, this aspect is also related to capital investment, for language and symbol systems are in part determined by the material environment. This happens through the adoption of textbooks, for instance, where the textbooks—as part of the material environment—help determine the symbol systems used by the students and teachers. The third aspect of the educative environment is the behaviors of the people in the environment (students, teachers and other school personnel). Again, this is related to capital investment in that there is a relationship between financial resources and the allocation of human resources. Huebner characterizes the human interactive aspect of educational environments as consisting of "symbolic skills, skills of coordinating human action and speech with material, and the habits and skills necessary for social interaction" (p. 222). Apple (1973) provides perhaps the clearest and most concise summary of this conception when he says:

> consider curriculum not as a thing, a reified object ... but as a *problem of designing an environment with manifold dimensions. Among these dimensions are symbol and information systems, the physical environment of buildings and furniture, material and technological aspects such as books, laboratory equipment, cameras, etc., personal aspects such as teacher skills and other students and personnel, and theoretical*

and metatheoretical dimensions such as the very language systems we use to talk about, order, and guide our activity ... [T]o these must be added for consideration power, organizational and ideological aspects.

(p. 168, original emphasis)

In addition to those outlined in "The Tasks of the Curricular Theorist," if we turn to other work by Huebner, we can add fourth, fifth, and sixth aspects of the educative environment. The fourth is that of time, or "temporality" in Huebner's words, in relation to the curriculum and educative environments. Temporality is important to understanding the curriculum as a problem of complex environmental design in three interrelated ways. First, there is a recognition of historicity in the design of educative environments. Huebner (1966) comments that:

> In most situations, the responsible person is confronted by a situation which has a past and a future. [Their] actions are limited and partially prescribed by the past and those factors which seem to be shaping the future. In other words, the actions of the curriculum person are historically determined. This is not an historical determination in a general, social sense ... Rather [they are] a participant in the evolution of a particular situation ...
>
> *(p. 6)*

To think about the design of educational environments is to acknowledge that the environments themselves are in part inherited. In that regard it is necessary to examine the specificity (historical or otherwise) of the environments we seek to influence and shape through the curriculum. The second reason that temporality is important is related to the first, in that it recognizes the role that the future plays in the development of educative environments and thus openly sees *possibility* in the act of learning. Huebner (1966) addresses this issue as follows:

> Educational conditions are incarnate educational possibilities, sometimes hidden from view, but awaiting the creative touch of the visionary who can imagine these possibilities coming to life in appropriate contexts. The designed educational environment is a fusion of given conditions and vision—it is the creation of meaning.
>
> *(p. 18)*

The temporality of educative environments, then, is not only historically situated, it is also deeply connected to the possible futures that may extend from those environments. This leads us to the third reason that temporality is important: if we recognize that the curriculum and the educative environments are rooted in the past and simultaneously oriented towards the possibility of a future, then we also recognize that the curriculum and educative environments are always developing, always in motion, and always in process. As Huebner (1966) states:

The designed environment is the answer of the curriculum leader to the available conditions. The conditions change as changes take place in the broader social-technological order. If the designed environment is to stay viable then it must grow and change with the changing conditions. That is, it must remain vital—almost alive as it reflects the growth of man and his environment. There can never be *the* curriculum; or the unchanging educational environment. The curriculum must always be in process.

(p. 19, original emphasis)

So far, within Huebner's conception of curriculum as a problem of environmental design, we've covered four aspects: materials, symbols, people, and time (including past, future, and continuous movement). Like the previous four, the fifth and sixth aspects are also interrelated in that, in Huebner's (1999b) terms, they are issues connected to "human events":

The practitioner can be considered a designer of educational environments for human events. This is a two-fold design problem. The first is an esthetic problem of composing the environment in such a way that events flow in valued ways … The second is a political design problem. Fabrication of educational environments is essentially social policy, involving people with different values and intentions. Reaching agreements about the characteristics of a particular environment requires a potential conflict among those con-cerned and the use of power to shape the environment. The resolution of conflict and the organization of power is essentially a problem of political design.

(Huebner, 1999b, p. 226)

Thus we see that, fifth, the design of educational environments has an artistic/creative aspect to it, in that the designer is essentially attempting to create an environment that is a connected whole where "events flow in valued ways" in order to make meaning. Sixth, we see that the designing of educative environments is indeed a matter of social policy, in that there is the potential for conflict and disagreement among participants as well. Values and intentions are also socially situated and therefore usher in issues of social and institutional power.

Huebner, like others before and after him, is hesitant to offer firm definitions. He remarks that, "[d]efinitions are again a stage along the way, not the beginning points. To attempt to define *educative environment* would immediately draw forth old solutions and arguments rather than push us to new levels" (Huebner, 1999b, p. 221, original emphasis). Instead, he, much as I have done thus far, offers *conceptions* of educational environments, and therefore suggests that:

[T]he school or classroom environment may be conceived as an aggregate of conditions which educate. The curriculum person is concerned with the nature of these conditions and their integration into an environment which reflects the values of those controlling education.

(Huebner, 1966, p. 2)

In this regard, Huebner goes on to conceptualize the curriculum as knowledge embodied in environmental form in ways to make it accessible to learners, and remarks that, "The building of environmental forms ... can be interpreted as the embodiment of information processing systems into the environment ... " (Huebner, 1970, p. 7). Thus, a strength of conceptualizing the curriculum as a problem of complex environmental design (one that is central to the arguments presented here) is in the powerful recognition that the structure of the educational environment around the learner has implications for the acquisition of knowledge by that learner. For Huebner (1999b), the tasks of the curricular theorist include: a "focus ... on the characteristics of the educative environment" (p. 222), "the development of a descriptive language ... to catalog and chart the environmental dimensions of practice" (p. 222), seeing "these educative environments in historical perspective" (p. 223), the articulation of "the development of the environmental components within a specific situation" (p. 223), and the "renewal and creation of environmental conditions" (p. 224), all of which aid us in understanding educative environments. To recap the outlines of Huebner's conception of the curriculum as a problem of environmental design, I offer the following summary:

1. There are six related aspects to any educational environment: (1) materials, (2) symbols, (3) people, (4) temporality (including past, future, and continuous movement), (5) art/creativity, and (6) politics.
2. The first three have direct relationships to material investment.
3. All six are directly connected to society either through the social construction of knowledge/values or through the social relations implied by education.
4. The educational environment may be conceived of as the aggregate of conditions that educate.
5. The curriculum, as situated in an educational environment, may be conceived of as the accessibility of knowledge in environmental form.
6. In turn, this conception shapes the tasks of the curricular theorist as: analyzing environmental characteristics, developing language for that analysis, understanding the educative environment historically, situating the development of those characteristics within specific contexts, and renewing and creating environmental conditions.

To conceive of the curriculum as the accessibility of knowledge embodied in environmental form recognizes that "accessibility" is a relative and power-laden term, one that raises three interrelated questions: (1) What knowledge is made accessible in the curriculum? (2) Who is allowed access to that knowledge? and (3) Who has the power to define the answers to these two questions? These questions point to a tacit relationship between the structure of knowledge in the curriculum, including how and to whom the curriculum makes this knowledge accessible.

Huebner's (1966, 1970, 1999a, 1999b) conception of the curriculum as the accessibility of knowledge embedded in environmental form is clearly connected to the dialectical conception of consciousness. Three of his six related aspects of the curriculum (specifically materials, people, and temporality) represent a commitment to philosophical materialism, which recognizes the importance of concrete conditions, social relations, and historical context in how we make sense of and interact with the world—and perhaps, even how the world is defined *for* us through external, environmental conditions. Three other aspects of curriculum discussed by Huebner (specifically symbols, art/creativity, and politics) speak to the relative autonomy of humans as they dialectically interact with and upon, as well in response to, their environments. Taken as a whole, even if he didn't explicitly frame it as such, these commitments to a dialectical conception of consciousness (as discussed in Chapter 2) are illustrated through Huebner's sense of curriculum as the accessibility of knowledge in environmental form.

The Curriculum as a Tool in the Activity of Accessing Knowledge

While I think that various aspects of Huebner's (1966, 1970, 1999a, 1999b) conception are central to how we think about what curriculum "is" relative to issues like the political economy of investment in education and the politics of knowledge, I would like to focus on what I have identified above as the fifth part of Huebner's framing: The curriculum, as situated in an educational environment, may be conceived of as the accessibility of knowledge in environmental form. To add to this conception, I would like to revisit Vygotsky (1987) and a series of points I made in the previous chapter.

In my discussion of the dialectical conception of consciousness in Chapter 2, I argued that consciousness is part and parcel with human individual and social (cultural) interaction with their environments (of which humans and human societies are also an active part). In making this argument I outlined how praxis—the dialectical unification of thinking and doing—is an essential part of how we conceive of our interactions with our environment. I then went on to highlight how, extending Engels' (1940) discussion of human evolution using physical tools, Vygotsky (1987) conceived of human development and learning vis-à-vis the use of conceptual/cultural tools, such as language, as humans dialectically interacted with the entirety of their environments. It is at this juncture of consciousness, praxis, and the use of tools where the work of both Huebner (1966, 1970, 1999a, 1999b) and Vygotsky (1987) are critical, particularly in terms of how we come to define and understand what curriculum is, as well as its function relative to the politics of how we learn about the world.

Vygotsky's (1987) framing of tools and environmental interaction is particularly important within the context of how we think about the curriculum. If we combine

Vygotsky's recognition of the role of tools (conceptual and otherwise) in learning and human development with Huebner's (1966, 1970, 1999a, 1999b) conception of curriculum, then we can move towards a synthesis of the two that adds a critical aspect to how we think about curriculum and consciousness: The curriculum includes the *tools* that we use to structure the accessibility of knowledge in environmental form. Re-conceiving of the curriculum in this way creates certain potentials in how we understand and define the curriculum.

For instance, by re-conceiving the curriculum in this manner, we can understand it as a multifaceted tool used to structure how knowledge is accessed through an educational environment. And to be clear, this thing-ness is not only found in the concrete objects, like books, other reading materials, art, desk arrangement, posters, etc. It has other dimensions as well. Pedagogic discourse itself, as well as the ensemble of relations that constitute classroom life, also becomes a part of the curriculum-as-tool, because the communication between students and teachers contributes to how knowledge is accessed in the educational environment. In this sense, different pedagogies—from lectures to inquiry to role plays, etc.—structure the accessibility of curricular knowledge in particular ways (Au, 2009a). Further, concepts are also a part of the curriculum-as-tool, because the very ideas students grapple with in their classes, the concepts with which they engage and use as they learn about the world, function to structure what knowledge they access and how they access it. Indeed, such a re-conception of the curriculum in this manner takes into account the various aspects and definitions of the curriculum (e.g., hidden, null, and enacted curriculum), discussed earlier in this chapter. In formulating the curriculum-as-tool, however, I must emphasize that I am not conceiving of the curriculum as a reified "thing." Rather, as I've explained here, the "tool"-ness of the curriculum includes processes and relations and thus should not be simplistically construed as a stagnant, ossified, physical tool.

When we look at the curriculum as a tool for the activity of accessing knowledge structured in educational environments, it also allows us to see how this tool functions differently for teachers and students in educational environments. For the classroom teacher, the curriculum serves as the tool for the activity of shaping how knowledge is accessed on the whole: Teachers use the curriculum to structure the educational environment of their classrooms in particular ways, to make particular knowledge and ways of understanding the world (epistemologies) accessible for student understanding, engagement, and potential action. In this sense teachers use the curriculum as a tool for the development of certain forms of consciousness and praxis amongst students.

To be clear, in asserting this point about how teachers use curriculum I am making a very specific argument, one that I think applies to all teachers (officially in schools or unofficially in communities) and all curricula, and this argument does not necessarily have anything to do with the politics of teaching and education per se. For instance, a math teacher who, without any particularly overtly or purposefully political approach to pedagogy, attempts to help a student grasp a basic mathematical function like addition or subtraction, uses their curriculum as a tool to structure that student's experience in the educational environment so that the student may access the knowledge of how to understand and use that basic mathematical function. The same could be said for students learning any discrete skill or concept or piece of information for any subject. Similarly, the point I am making here also holds true for any pedagogy—teacher-centered lecture, student-centered inquiry, etc. The key is to see that different pedagogies simply alter what knowledge is made accessible within an educational environment, as well as how that knowledge is accessed.

However, understanding the curriculum-as-a-tool allows us to see the distinct difference in the ways that students interact with and make use of this tool. As opposed to the teacher's use of curriculum to structure the accessibility of knowledge in the educational environment—where the curriculum as a whole functions as the tool for the teacher, the student has another relationship to the curriculum. For the student, the tools are embedded in the curriculum and consist of the concepts, activities, readings, classroom relations, etc., that they end up using to access knowledge in environmental form. In a most basic sense, the teacher uses the curriculum to structure the environment and the interactive processes such structure implicates, whereas the student uses the curriculum to access the knowledge in the environmental structure. Clearly they are two, related parts of the same process, but also are undoubtedly different. Indeed, we might loosely map this onto the difference between teaching and learning (taking for granted, of course, that good teachers learn from their students, and that all students teach both each other and their teachers). Further, we might also say in the abstract that any teaching, purposefully or otherwise, structures environments to selectively make certain knowledge accessible to certain learners. And we also might say that such attempts, purposefully or otherwise, simultaneously make certain knowledge inaccessible to some learners too.

Curriculum-as-Tool, Pedagogic Discourse, and the Shaping of Consciousness

The issue still remains, however, as to how the curriculum-as-tool is operationalized in educational environments. Bernstein's (1977, 1996) work in pedagogic discourse helps address this. For Bernstein, pedagogic discourse consists of the communication of cultural codes, including what he refers to as the classification and framing of knowledge in the classroom. Classification, Bernstein (1996) explains, is:

> the crucial space which creates the specialization of the category—in this case the discourse—is not internal to that discourse but is the space between that discourse and another. In other words, A can only be A if it can effectively insulate itself from B. In this sense, there is no A if there is no relationship between A and something else. The meaning of A is only understandable in relation to other categories in the set. ... In other words, it is silence which carries the message of power; it is the full stop between one category of discourse and another; it is the dislocation in the potential flow of discourse which is

crucial to the specialization of any category. If that insulation is broken, then a category is in danger of losing its identity, because what it is, is the space between it and another category. Whatever maintains the strengths of the insulation, maintains the relations between the categories ... Thus, the principle of the relations between categories, discourses—that is, the principles of their social division of labour—is a function of the degree of insulation between the categories ...

(pp. 20–21).

As a more concrete, curriculum-related example to illustrate Bernstein's above point, take the subject areas of social studies and language arts in some of the public high schools in which I have taught. Classification refers to the boundary between these subject areas—the space between them that insulates them from each other. In one public high school in which I taught, there existed a social studies department completely separate from the language arts department, and the social studies and language arts courses reflected this distinction: Students could only take social studies and language arts classes that were individually distinct from each other (and teacher could only teach such distinct courses). In this public high school, the form of the curriculum communicated a clear classification between these subjects, and in this example Bernstein would say that these subjects/courses were strongly classified. That is to say, that the forms that subject/courses took manifested in thick insulation from each other: There were strong boundaries between them.

Where I used to teach, at Middle College High School (discussed in Chapter 1), however, social studies and language arts had a very different relationship. There, social studies and language arts were completely integrated. I taught the class with another instructor, and the curricular form our course took completely meshed social studies and language arts together into one seamless, whole subject: Humanities. In a Bernsteinian (1977, 1996) sense, the curricular form of the humanities course I co-taught did not delineate a distinct classification between social studies and language arts, even though we gave separate social studies and language arts credits. There was virtually no insulation or boundary between these two subjects (which are usually clearly separated or bounded in most schools). Bernstein would say that in my humanities course, there was weak and perhaps no classification at all between the social studies and language arts: The boundary between these two individual subjects was so transparent, the insulation so thin, that their formal identity as distinct, individual social studies and language arts courses functionally ceased to exist—so much so that we reconceived the course under a category of "humanities" instead.

For Bernstein (1996), framing is the complement to classification. He explains that, "Classification refers to *what*, framing is concerned with *how* meanings are to be put together, the forms by which they are to be made public, and the nature of the social relationships that go with it" (p. 27, original emphasis). He also explains that "[F]raming refers to the controls on communication in local, interactional pedagogic relations: between parents/children, teacher/pupil, social worker/client, etc … " (p. 26). In this sense, while classification refers to the boundaries between things as a function of identity maintenance (which could loosely be understood as how knowledge is organized or compartmentalized into relatively distinct categories), framing refers to how those boundaries are communicated in pedagogic discourse (literally how knowledge is communicated within the entirety of discourse that takes place in the classroom or other educational settings). Framing is thus about the selection of knowledge, its sequencing, its pacing, the criteria of selection, and the social/educational interactions that communicate that knowledge—implicating both *how* meaning is communicated and *who* has control over what happens in classroom discourse (Bernstein, 1996; Morais, 2002). Framing is the communication of classification.

To provide a simple illustration of framing, I'll return to my above example of the teaching of the social studies and language arts. In the high school I used to teach in where social studies and language arts were more distinct and separated from each other (strongly classified), social studies class was for the teaching of social studies, just as language arts was for the teaching of language arts. This distinction manifested in the pedagogic discourse of the classroom: The knowledge selected for social studies, as well as its pacing, criteria of selection, and the classroom interactions used to communicate that knowledge, generally only embodied the social studies in terms of content and teaching objectives. The same could be said of the language arts classrooms. In its most simple form, what this meant is that when a particular era of history was taught in the social studies, literature was rarely (if ever) used to inform how history was taught, nor was historical context rarely (if ever) used to inform the teaching of specific novels in the language arts classes. The strong classification between social studies and language arts was framed (communicated) through how those subjects were taught in the individual social studies and language arts classrooms.

The exact opposite was true for my experience teaching a social studies/language arts integrated humanities course at Middle College High School. In that humanities course we always used literature to inform the social studies, just as we always used historical context to inform our reading of literature. The weak classification between the social studies and language arts in our humanities course was framed (communicated) through our consistent integration of these two subject areas. We never taught social studies separate from language arts, or vice versa. Social studies always included the human perspectives carried in writing, just as language arts was always about humans expressing themselves in particular historical and social contexts: Both subjects were continually used to make sense of each other, and we framed that relationship through our pedagogic discourse—in our day-to-day classroom communication.

Bernstein's conceptualization of classification and framing helps explain the process of how curriculum operates as the tool that structures the accessibility of knowledge in environmental form. Classification, with its attention to the form that curricular knowledge takes, essentially points to the structure of knowledge as it is bounded and organized in environmental form. Framing, with its attention to how such knowledge is communicated through the entirety of pedagogic discourse— the communication that literally frames the educational experiences of learners— subsequently points to how knowledge is accessed, as pedagogic discourse functions to selectively make knowledge accessible. In this way classification and framing help clarify the relationship between the knowledge structured in environmental form and how it is accessed vis-à-vis the curriculum.

Thus, in sum, the curriculum can be conceived of as the tool that structures the accessibility of knowledge in environmental form, where framing and classification, respectively, communicate the accessibility and structure of knowledge embedded in the environment. In making this summary statement, however, I want to explicitly caution against conceiving of curriculum as a reified "thing." Instead, in this conception of curriculum, we have to understand that "tool" does not just refer to a physical tool (which it may in the form of actual reading materials, etc.), but rather to also understand that concepts, classroom activities, and classroom relations are tools as well. Indeed, as Bernstein's (1996) and Vygotsky's (1987) work both highlight, the conception of curriculum I've developed here should be understood as embodying an ensemble of relations: relations between learners and environments and each other and themselves and teachers/facilitators, amongst all the "things" in the curricular environment. Indeed, these "things" represent processes and relations themselves that exist amidst the amalgam of educational policies and practices that all educational environments coalesce.

High-Stakes Testing and the Control of Educational Environments

To more concretely illustrate this conception of curriculum as the tool that structures the accessibility of knowledge in environmental form, the structure and accessibility of which are organized and communicated through classification and framing, I'll draw upon the example of high-stakes, standardized testing—a subject I've dealt with at length in previous research and analyses (see, e.g., Au, 2009f).

Since being implemented as the central lever for education reform in the United States vis-à-vis the No Child Left Behind Act (Au, 2010a; Natriello & Pallas, 2001), high-stakes, standardized testing has exerted significant levels of control over the curriculum. Specifically, in response to the tests, teachers, schools, and districts have increasingly restricted their course offerings to expand the tested subjects of reading and mathematics, teachers have increasingly turned to teacher-centered lecture formats to deliver tested content, and that teachers are changing the very form in which they present knowledge in order to match that required by the tests (Au, 2007b). Indeed, we can see very clearly from the body of research that standardized, high-stakes testing creates stronger classification between tested and non-tested content, as well as creating strong framing in how such content is communicated in pedagogic discourse (Au, 2008c, 2009f), as teachers increasingly either resort to or are required to teach to the tests to raise scores (Au, 2007b, 2011).

In a most basic and general sense then, high-stakes testing has become the curriculum: The tests have, with increasing intensity, become the tool for structuring educational environments in ways that also shape both what knowledge is accessed and how that knowledge is accessed through pedagogic discourse. As a result, educational environments have become less rich in terms of content as field trips, art, music, recess, physical education, social studies, and any other educational experiences that aren't on the tests are eroded in favor of more testing, more practice for testing, and more time spent on tested subjects alone (Au, 2007b, 2009e, 2009f).

It is important to consider that the way the tests structure knowledge in environmental form and shape how that knowledge is accessed not only directly impact the material realities and relations of classroom instruction, but also the identities of both students and teachers. The learner identities being made available to students are limited within the test-influenced educational environments because multicultural education and communities and cultures that do not fall within the standard defined norms are not reflected in the curriculum (Au, 2009d; McNeil, 2000; Valenzuela, 2005b). Teachers' identities are experiencing what Ball (2003b, 2006) refers to as the "terrors of performativity" as their identities are being limited and defined by the tests themselves (Au, 2011)—a testament to how teachers are also being taught by the educational environments structured by the tests-as-curricular-tool.

Bernstein (1996) refers to the control of student identities through the curriculum in terms of a distribution of images, where he remarks:

> A school metaphorically holds up a mirror in which an image is reflected. There may be several images, positive and negative. A school's ideology may be seen as a construction in a mirror through which images are reflected. The question is: who recognizes themselves as of value? What other images are excluded by the dominant image of value so that some students are unable to recognize themselves?
>
> *(p. 7)*

High-stakes, standardized tests literally structure the knowledge embedded in educational environments as well as shape the accessibility of that knowledge in ways that selectively validate and invalidate the identities of students and teachers.

Power Relations in the Structure and Accessibility of Knowledge

The above two points regarding how high-stakes testing acts a tool for both structuring how knowledge is embedded in educational environments and how that knowledge is accessed also illustrate a more basic point: The curriculum and the structure of knowledge are fundamentally an expression of social, economic, and political power relations. When we understand the curriculum as the accessibility of knowledge structured into educational environments, as Huebner (1970) explains:

> [When] educators concern themselves with the accessibility and distribution of knowledge, they also concern themselves with the accessibility and distribution of power. The social distribution of rationality is related to the social distribution of power ... The accessibility of some knowledge is more dangerous than the accessibility of other knowledge.
>
> *(p. 14)*

Bernstein concurs, and explains that power and control are explicit within the classification and framing of knowledge, and that both are connected to social relations:

> [V]ariations in the distribution of power (classifications) and variations in the principles of control (framings) impose or enable variations in the formation of identities and their change, through differential specialisation of communication and of its social base.
>
> *(Bernstein & Solomon, 1999, p. 271)*

Elsewhere, Bernstein (1996) observes that "[C]lassifications, strong or weak, always carry power relations" (p. 21). Evidence to support both Huebner and Bernstein, such as my earlier example of high-stakes testing, abounds, but to further illustrate I'll draw upon research on systems of tracking and the process of de-tracking.

Tracking is the practice of sorting students based on perceived abilities or occupational goals (Oakes, 2005). Chunn (1987–88) finds four rationalizations undergirding systems of tracking:

- Students learn better when grouped with academically similar students.
- "Slower" students develop high esteem for themselves and their schools if not placed together with more "capable" students.
- The sorting process is "accurate and fair" and mirrors previous achievement and "innate abilities."
- Teachers can more easily work with homogeneous groups of students.

There are basically two types of tracking: "curriculum tracking" and "ability grouping." Curriculum tracking is the practice of using specific educational programs, like vocational, general, and/or college prep classes as a means of dividing students (Donelan, Neal, & Jones, 1994; Gamoran, 1992). Ability grouping is commonly used to determine which level of a particular subject a student takes, or is used to create small ability groups within a heterogeneously grouped classroom (Broussard & Joseph, 1998; Gamoran, 1992).

Regardless of the specific type, research has found that tracking generally results in a disparity of educational opportunity and resources that mimics the social, economic, and racial inequalities that exist outside of schooling (Oakes, 2005). Stated more simply, tracking reproduces social and educational inequality. This tracking induced inequality has spurred many schools to de-track their courses, programs, and schools (Au, 2005; Bigelow, 1994). Such de-tracking, however, has also drawn significant resistance. Anecdotally, I experienced both the push to de-track and the subsequent resistance it evoked when I was a public high-school history teacher in the city of Berkeley, California. One set of teachers, a stereotypical group of older, White males who comprised less than a fourth of the history department, actively worked towards creating a special, elite, small school-within-a-school for Advanced Placement students at Berkeley High. The overwhelming majority of the teachers in our department and school were against it, and a clear decision was made against this elitist program. We were committed to a de-tracked history department and a de-tracked school, and as teachers we were committed to educational equity. Ultimately such commitments didn't matter. With the help of affluent Berkeley parents, this cabal of teachers applied pressure with the district and established their elite small school despite the professional, more equitable decision made by the teachers. These elitist parents and teachers were able to push their inequitable program despite all of the known issues with such educational tracking.

Ethnographic research has found that privileged parents often intervene advantageously on behalf of their children regardless if it is in opposition to the decisions of school personnel (Lucas, 1999) or even if it may prove academically harmful to other children (Brantlinger, 2003). To explain this phenomenon, Oakes, Welner, Yonezawa, and Allen (1998) frame schools as "zones of mediation" between community norms/tolerances and education policy. In their research, White middle and upper class parents balked at "equity minded" school reforms like heterogeneous grouping because they were angered that their children might lose the social and cultural power identified with high-level classes. In the minds of these parents, their children's ability to enter into an elite college depended upon their children's academic transcripts, transcripts that had to signal that their children had taken elite courses. Such attendance to their children's credentials despite the ramifications for the education of marginalized groups illustrates how tracking and other forms of educational differentiation serve as mechanisms for socio-economic class reproduction and vehicles for upward mobility for privileged groups (Apple, 2006; Bernstein, 1996). Many of these same tensions exist relative to systems of high-stakes testing as well (Au, 2008a).

Systems of tracking, and privileged parents' resistance to dismantling tracking, illustrate both Huebner's point about the accessibility of knowledge being connected to the social distribution of power as well as Bernstein's (1996) point about classification (and by implication, framing) being tied to power relations. Although on the surface tracking would seem to be purely a policy issue, it is also curricular in nature. Through the grouping of students in different forms and levels of classes, in a Huebnerian (1970) sense, tracking results in the differential distribution of and access to knowledge to different groups of students. This differential distribution and access results in the formation of "high" track and "low" track students, where "high" track students generally have increased educational resources at their disposal as well as an increased likelihood to attend college and experience upward socio-economic mobility (Oakes, 2005). Thus, in a Bernsteinian (1996) sense, tracked educational settings exhibit strong classification between "high" track and "low" track students, with a thickly insulated boundary existing in the curricular form of the two general categories. This strong classification is subsequently communicated (framed) in pedagogic discourse vis-à-vis the differential access to knowledge different students experience depending on which curricular track they may be. It is this differential curriculum and experience that works to reproduce socio-economic class relations by increasing the likelihood that privileged students will be more upwardly mobile than less privileged students. Following Bourdieu (1984), Apple (2006) explains:

> The increasing power of mechanisms of restratification ... enhance the chances that the children of the professional and managerial new middle class will have *less competition* from other students. Thus, the introduction of devices to restratify a population ... enhances the value of credentials that the new middle class is more likely given to accumulate, given the stock of cultural capital it already possesses.
>
> *(pp. 106–7, original emphasis)*

It is the differentiation between students produced by tracking (and other educational systems and policies such as high-stakes testing) that enables student X to be identified as better credentialed and therefore more deserving than student Y, ultimately justifying student X's upward mobility and class position. That systems of tracking have produced student grouping that effectively parallels race and class groupings that exist socio-economically only further illustrates how power relations reach into the curriculum.

The movement to de-track and the subsequent resistance from privileged communities further illustrate how power exists in the structure and accessibility of curricular knowledge. Fundamentally, de-tracking the curriculum does two things simultaneously. First it collapses the distinction between "high" and "low" track student groups. Second, it more equally distributes the accessibility of knowledge across all groups of students. In a Bernsteinian (1996) sense, de-tracking functionally weakens the classification both between groups of students and the form curriculum takes.

Such weakened classification, however, raises significant problems for the socio-economic class reproduction of privileged groups because it functionally challenges one significant way their children are distinguished from those of more marginalized communities: You cannot say student X has a stronger pedigree or more valuable credential than student Y if there is no system in place to create such differentiation, no way to establish a thick boundary relation between groups of students. Thus, parents from privileged communities have sometimes fought to resist more equitable educational reforms like de-tracking because such reforms functionally decrease their children's chances to distinguish themselves from other students—simultaneously decreasing their children's chances at upward mobility in a highly competitive educational "marketplace." It is through such resistance to equitable change that we see how the form curriculum takes—the structure and accessibility of knowledge— is connected to power relations; that to reiterate Huebner's (1970) above point, "As educators concern themselves with the accessibility and distribution of knowledge, they also concern themselves with the accessibility and distribution of power" (p. 14); or that, as Bernstein (1996) observes, "Attempts to change degrees of insulation reveal the power relations on which the classification is based and which it repro- duces ... " (p. 21). Indeed, one could argue that the hidden curriculum (Anyon, 1980; Apple, 2004; Margolis et al., 2001) and the reproduction of social relations that the concept describes are a manifestation of "the accessibility and distribution of power" through variable "accessibility and distribution of knowledge" (Huebner, 1970, p. 14) to different groups, the distinction between which are based on strongly classified boundaries of social and curricular stratification.

Conclusion

In this chapter I developed a conception of curriculum that aligned with the dialectical conception of consciousness outlined in Chapter 2. To do so I reviewed some of the prominent, historical definitions of curriculum within the field of curriculum studies, touched upon the work of Dewey (1901, 1916), and ultimately identified Huebner's (1966, 1970, 1999a, 1999b) elaboration of curriculum as a problem of complex environmental design as one consistent with my earlier formulation of humans interacting dialectically with their environments in the process of learning. I then incorporated the work of Vygotsky (1987) to posit the role that tools play in this environmental interaction, a conceptual move that allowed for the discussion of how curricular tools for teachers and students differ categorically and functionally. I further drew upon Bernstein's (1996) work on classification (structure of knowl- edge) and framing (how that knowledge is communicated) to elaborate on the relationship between curricular environmental design and the accessibility of knowledge vis-à-vis pedagogic discourse. Ultimately, and in sum, *the curriculum can be conceived of as the tool that structures the accessibility of knowledge in environmental form, where framing and classification, respectively, communicate the accessibility and structure of knowledge.*

I continued my analysis and theory development with a brief concrete example of the ways in which high-stakes, standardized tests structure educational environments in particular ways as well as place limits on the accessibility of knowledge in those environments. Finally, using tracking and de-tracking as an example, I concluded with a discussion of how conceiving the curriculum as the accessibility of knowledge in environmental form also recognizes that socio-economic power relations manifest in the curriculum.

In a general sense, the theoretical and conceptual formulation I have outlined in this chapter serves as a bridge. Looking back, conceiving of the curriculum as tool (in a non-reified sense) that structures the accessibility of knowledge in environmental form is simply an extension of the dialectical conception of consciousness I detailed in Chapter 2. Looking forward, the conception of curriculum foreshadows a more detailed discussion of the politics of the curriculum, as well as how those politics relate to consciousness. It is to the politics of the curriculum that I now turn the focus in Chapter 4.

[1] Dialectical conception of consciousness.
[2] ↳ Formulation of curriculum.

Social Relations ⟷ Consciousness
        ↳ Knowledge construction
        ↳ Access to Knowledge

struggle b/w dominant & subordinate gps

⟹ outcome impacts curriculum
    socially contested choices about content
        ↳ epistemological orientations (which of them are ligitimized).
        ✗ what is deemed sactioned/accepted
        made readily available to students.

⟹ Knowledge is inherently political
    social, cultural, economic contexts

⟹ Curricular Standpoint to combat status-quo hegemonic
    school knowledge functions to maintain & reproduce
    unequal social relations.

✱✱ Standpoint Theory as a methodological tool for
        ① curriculum inquiry
        ② = practice.

4

DEVELOPING CURRICULAR STANDPOINT: STRONG OBJECTIVITY AND THE POLITICS OF SCHOOL KNOWLEDGE

Introduction

Thus far in this book I have detailed a dialectical conception of consciousness, as well as a formulation of curriculum that this conception implicates. In the process I have pointed to, both explicitly and implicitly, a corollary between the two: Consciousness is fundamentally connected to social relations, and the way knowledge is structured and accessed in the curriculum is also connected to social relations. My formulation here follows and is an extension of Apple (1988), who explains that the curriculum takes "particular social forms and embodies certain interests which are themselves the outcomes of continuous struggles within and among dominant and subordinate groups" (p. 193). Thus, not only does curriculum imply socially contested choices about content, it also carries with it explicit and implicit messages about what epistemological orientations are deemed valuable and made readily available to students, as some groups' perspectives are sanctioned over others (Au & Apple, 2009a).

It is from this vantage, that knowledge is inherently political and requires struggle for epistemological legitimacy within our given social, cultural, and economic contexts, that I seek to construct an argument for what I am calling "curricular standpoint," as a political and epistemological intervention against status-quo, hegemonic school knowledge that, in our current system, functions to maintain and reproduce unequal social relations (Apple, 1995; Au, 2009f). In what follows, I begin by out-lining standpoint theory as originally conceived by Lukacs (1971), and then further developed by leading, critical, feminist scholars (Harding, 2004b; Hartsock, 1998a). I then consider how standpoint in various forms has been formally used (and mis-used) within educational research, and then conclude by developing a framework for curricular standpoint as a methodological tool for both curriculum inquiry and curricular practice.

Standpoint Theory

Standpoint theory formally originated with Lukacs (1971) and his elaboration of proletarian standpoint, a concept which he drew from an essay written by Marx in *The Holy Family* (Marx & Engels, 1956) which explains how the bourgeoisie (property owning class) and the proletariat (working class) experience alienation from the production of commodities under capitalism in qualitatively different ways:

> The property-owning class and the class of the proletariat represent the same human self-alienation. But the former feels at home in this self-alienation and feels itself confirmed by it; it recognizes alienation as its own instrument and in it possesses the semblance of a human existence. The latter feels itself destroyed by this alienation and sees in it its own impotence and the reality of an inhuman existence.
>
> *(Marx as cited in Lukacs, 1971, p. 149)*

Building on Marx's analysis of the differential alienation felt by owners and workers relative to capitalist production, Lukacs goes on to look at what this implies for the different perceptions on reality expressed by capitalists and workers:

> [F]or the worker the reified character of the immediate manifestations of capitalist society receives the most extreme definition possible. It is true: for the capitalist also there is the same doubling of personality, the same splitting up … into an element of the movement of commodities and an … observer of that moment. But for [their] consciousness it necessarily appears as an activity … in which effects emanate from [themselves]. This illusion blinds [them] to the true state of affairs, whereas the worker, who is denied the scope for such illusory activity, perceives the split in [their] being preserved in the brutal form of what is in its whole tendency a slavery without limits. [They are] therefore forced into becoming the object of the process by which [they are] turned into a commodity and reduced to a mere quantity.
>
> *(Lukacs, 1971, p. 166)*

In Lukacs' analysis, it is the process of capitalist production that turns workers into commodities/quantities, who, within capitalism, become objects of production (and, simultaneously, objects of history). Conversely, the capitalist, in their position of ownership, power, privilege, and control simply sees their subjective agency over production and life as "emanating from [themselves]." It is this subjective agency that thus "blinds [them] to the true state of affairs." Lukacs then extends this argument to literally take up how different methods of understanding the world are implicated by different class locations within capitalism, where he explains that:

> [E]very method is necessarily implicated in the existence of the relevant class. For the bourgeoisie, method arises directly from its social existence and this

means that mere immediacy adheres to its thought, constituting its outermost barrier, one that cannot be crossed. In contrast to this the proletariat is confronted by the need to break through this barrier, to overcome it inwardly *from the very start* by adopting its own point of view … [T]he proletariat finds itself *repeatedly* confronted with the problem of its own point of departure both in its efforts to increase its theoretical grasp of reality …

(Lukacs, 1971, p. 164, original emphasis)

In the 1970s and 80s critical feminist scholars, particularly those more strongly identified with Marxism, sought to use the framework provided by Lukacs' (1971) proletarian standpoint to develop a conception of feminist standpoint to challenge both masculinist norms and regressive gender politics found in research in the social and physical sciences (Benton & Craib, 2001; Harding, 2004a). Since then, standpoint theory—along with feminist studies more broadly—has struggled with its own internal politics of difference (e.g., issues of race, class, nationality, and sexuality), and concepts of U.S. "third world" feminism—specifically "oppositional consciousness" (Sandoval, 2000), as well as Black feminist standpoint (Hill Collins, 1989), have contributed to the development of standpoint theory. In what follows I sketch an outline of standpoint theory, particularly of those theorists associated with more philosophically materialist conceptions (Benton & Craib, 2001), in order to argue the political and epistemological necessity of standpoint in the curriculum and in curriculum studies.

Standpoint theory builds from the basic understanding that power and knowledge are inextricably intertwined, that "they co-constitute and co-maintain each other" (Harding, 2004a, p. 67), and that this power relation is socially situated because,

For any particular interpretive context, new knowledge claims must be consistent with an existing body of knowledge that the group controlling the interpretive context accepts as true. The methods used to validate knowledge claims must also be acceptable to the group controlling the knowledge-validation process.

(Hill Collins, 1989, p. 753)

Thus, as an extension of the control over validated knowledge, methodologically and epistemologically speaking, standpoint theory also operates under the assumption that "there are some perspectives on society from which … the real relations of humans with each other and with the natural world are not visible" (Hartsock, 1998a, p. 107) both because of the differential power relations relative to knowledge production and because of the epistemological limits carried with the viewpoint provided by specific social locations.

As it has been articulated by Hartsock (1998a) and Harding (2004a, 2004b), standpoint theory consists of five central themes that guide it epistemologically and methodologically:

- First, standpoint theory asserts that our material experiences—social relations included—structure our epistemology of the world in ways that both limit and enable certain ways of understanding (Harding, 2004a; Hartsock, 1998a). That is to say, our social locations both enable us to see and understand the world more clearly with respect to our positionality *and* make our ability to understand the world beyond that same positionality more difficult. However, it is critical to acknowledge that making this point does not mean that one cannot understand someone else's socially located epistemology. Rather, the point is to say that the socially located epistemologies of others may be more difficult to grasp and wouldn't necessarily be a part of one's commonsense understanding of the world.

- Second, because our experience and material life are embedded in and structured by systems of domination and rule that are organized hierarchically around power relations of race, class, gender, sexuality, nationality, and other forms of socially determined categorical difference, the epistemologies available to groups in power contradict and run counter to the epistemologies of oppressed groups—forming epistemological inversions of each other (Harding, 2004a; Hartsock, 1998a). Put simply, by nature of their different experiences from within their social locations, the ruler's view of the world will in many ways be oppositional to that of the ruled.

- Third, because of differentials in power (and how such power manifests unequally in social, cultural, and political institutions), the perspectives of those in power are made functional in the lives of everyone regardless of position, because "the ruling group can be expected to structure the material relations in which all people are forced to participate" (Hartsock, 1998a, p. 229) as "all are forced to live in social structures and institutions designed to serve the oppressors' understandings of self and society" (Harding, 2004a, p. 68). Thus, the skewed understanding of the world that is imposed institutionally by those in power illustrates how "epistemology grows in a complex and contradictory way from material life," where a standpoint "explains the 'surface' or appearance, and indicates the logic by means of which the appearance inverts or distorts the deeper reality" (Hartsock, 1998a, p. 107). Put differently, we might say that the unequal distribution of power leads to the unequal distribution of epistemologies, where those with more power can exert stronger influence on our commonsense understandings of the world, even if such commonsense understandings fundamentally operate as distorted conceptions of material reality (Gramsci, 1971).

- Fourth, and as a consequence of the previous, a standpoint is always born of struggle against the hegemonic standpoint of those in power, making it an "achievement" that arises from active, conscious work against the reigning, oppressive, institutionalized epistemology. Subsequently a standpoint "must be struggled for against the apparent realities made 'natural' and 'obvious' by dominant institutions" (Harding, 2004a, p. 68), the activity of which "requires both systematic analysis and the education that can only grow from political struggle to change those relations" (Hartsock, 1998a, p. 229). As such, we can never assume that a standpoint is simply given by one's social location—just because one comes from a marginalized or oppressed social location does not mean that one automatically has taken up a standpoint: People from oppressed groups can and do maintain forms of consciousness that are regressive, just as people from dominant groups can also develop forms of consciousness that are progressive too. Rather, a standpoint arises from conscious, resistant struggle against the prevailing and hegemonic forms of oppressive consciousness.

- Fifth, the taking up of a standpoint by the oppressed and marginalized carries with it the potential for liberation because it "makes visible the inhumanity of relations among human beings" (Hartsock, 1998, p. 229), emphasizing that:

> An oppressed group must become a group "for itself," not just "in itself" in order for it to see the importance of engaging in political and scientific struggles to see the world from the perspective of its own lives.
>
> *(Harding, 2004a, pp. 68–69)*

This also necessarily requires the development of "oppositional consciousness" (Sandoval, 2000) as the oppressed create transformative epistemologies as part of their struggle against existing power relations. Indeed, this liberatory potential of standpoint makes it dangerous to the prevailing social order, and therefore gives cause for the more powerful to actively seek to discredit such positions (Hill Collins, 1989).

Standpoint, Epistemology, and Strong Objectivity

Fundamentally, as outlined above, standpoint theory argues that certain social locations, specifically those of women and other systematically oppressed or marginalized groups, provide the best "starting off thought" for generating "illuminating critical questions that do not arise in thought that begins from the dominant group lives" (Harding, 2004b, p. 128) because "marginalized lives are better places from which to start asking causal and critical questions about the social order" (p. 130). As Hartsock (1998a) explains,

> [T]he criteria for privileging some knowledges over others are ethical and political as well as purely "epistemological." The quotation marks here are to indicate that I see ethical and political concepts such as that of power as involving epistemological claims on the one hand, and ideas of what is to count as knowledge involving profoundly important political and ethical stakes on the other. Marx made an important claim that knowledge that takes its starting point from the lives of those who have suffered from exploitation produces better accounts of the world than that starting from the

lives of dominant groups ... [T]he view from the margins (defined in more heterogeneous terms) is clearer and better.

(p. 80)

Thus, social location provides an important epistemological standpoint because, not only does "the experience of domination ... provide the possibility of important new understandings of social life" (Hartsock, 1998a, p. 240), it also provides a sharper view of material and social relations.

From this perspective it follows that standpoint theory is not a singularly feminist project (at least as far as feminism being defined as solely being about "women's issues"). Rather, as Harding (2004b) explains,

> [T]he subject of liberatory feminist knowledge must also be, in an important if controversial sense, the subject of every other liberatory knowledge project. This is true in the collective sense of "subject of knowledge," because lesbian, poor, and racially marginalized women are all women, and therefore feminists will have to grasp how gender, race, and class, and sexuality are used to construct each other.
>
> *(p. 134)*

Standpoint theory thus invites a recognition of personhood and one's equality, which means that by definition it must also be connected to anti-racist and anti-homophobic positions, among others. Hence, standpoint has to contend with issues of power and oppression in a general sense, since, as a paradigmatic orientation, standpoint openly acknowledges that the social location of the oppressed and marginalized (as defined by historical, social, cultural, and institutional contexts) is the best vantage point for starting knowledge projects because it can provide a clearer, more truthful lens for understanding the world than that of hegemonic epistemologies.

To be clear, however, in making such arguments, standpoint theory does not argue for total epistemological relativity, where every socially located standpoint simply holds equal value relative to every other socially located standpoint. Rather, as Harding (2004b) asserts, standpoint theory

> argues against the idea that all social situations provide equally useful resources for learning about the world and against the idea that they all set equally strong limits on knowledge. ... Standpoint theory provides arguments for the claim that some social situations are scientifically better than others as places from which to start off knowledge projects ...
>
> *(p. 131)*

Thus, neither a call for epistemological relativism, nor "an empiricist appeal to or by 'the oppressed' ... ," a standpoint is perhaps better conceived as "a cognitive, psychological, and political tool for more adequate knowledge judged by the non-essentialist, historically contingent, situated standards of strong objectivity" (Haraway, 1991, as cited in Hartsock, 1998, p. 236). Such a tool allows for "the creation of better (more objective, more liberatory) accounts of the world" (Hartsock, 1998a, p. 236)—even if, as Harding (2004b) asserts, "The epistemologically advantaged starting points for research do not guarantee that the researcher can maximize objectivity in her account; these grounds provide only a necessary—not sufficient—starting point for maximizing objectivity" (p. 128).

On a simple reading, it might seem contradictory that an epistemological and methodological model such as standpoint, one that essentially emphasizes a specific type of subjectivity related to social location, relies so heavily on concepts of objectivity—either in the form of Hartsock's (1998a) references to "more objective" perspectives on the world or what Harding (2004b) and Haraway (1991) refer to as "strong objectivity." In reality, there is no contradiction in these scholars' formulations, as they recognize that there is a material world outside of human subjectivity that can in fact be understood, and that such understanding takes place dialectically, through interaction and mutual reaction between humans and their environments (Allman, 2007)—much in line with the dialectical conception of consciousness outlined in Chapter 2. Hence, standpoint argues that we can achieve *more* objective understandings of that objectively existing world by not only recognizing the subjectivity in our epistemology, but by also embracing our subjectivity consciously and actively reflecting on it within our socio-political environments (as well as actively reflecting upon the process of "knowing" itself). Harding (2004b) puts it thusly:

> Strong objectivity requires that the subject of knowledge be placed on the same critical, causal plane as the objects of knowledge. Thus, strong objectivity requires what we can think of as "strong reflexivity." This is because culturewide (or nearly culturewide) beliefs function as evidence at every stage of scientific inquiry: in the selection of problems, the formation of hypotheses, the design of research (including the organization of research communities), the collection of data, the interpretation and sorting of data, decisions about when to stop research, the way results of research are reported, and so on. The subject of knowledge—the individual and the historically located social community whose unexamined beliefs its members are likely to hold "unknowingly," so to speak—must be considered as part of the object of knowledge from the perspective of scientific method.
>
> *(p. 136)*

Strong objectivity means that we gain a better, clearer, and more truthful—more strongly objective—understanding of social and material realities from the achievement of a standpoint in our knowledge projects because we "can take the subject as well as the object of knowledge to be a necessary object of critical, causal—scientific!—social explanations" (Harding, 2004b, p. 137). Standpoint theory thus provides a particularly robust justification for taking up a critical politics in our teaching, as well as a strong framework for understanding the politics of knowledge in the curriculum.

Standpoint in Educational Research

Standpoint theory has been used sparingly in educational research. Some of the earliest applications arose within the milieu of the development of feminist pedagogies that challenged heterosexual, patriarchal norms of classroom interactions and sought to emphasize women's narratives and points of view as critical entry points into a deeper and more full understanding of the world (Manicom, 1992; Weiler, 1991). Since then, standpoint theory has been discussed in relation to educational research generally, as well as applied to a smattering of educational research projects. In terms of general discussions focusing on educational research, Greene (1994) for instance, briefly touches upon the concept of standpoint theory in her review of contributions to shifting epistemologies in educational research, and Denzin and Lincoln (2000) see standpoint theory as contributing new perspectives to the body of qualitative educational research. Howe (2009) further highlights standpoint theory as an important challenge to issues associated with objectivist dogma found in positivist paradigms of scientific research, and Glasser & Smith III (2008) note that standpoint theory, as a manifestation of what they refer to as "materialist accounts of gender" (p. 346), is used as one analytic framework research on how the terms "gender" and "sex" are often conflated in educational scholarship. Foley, Levinson, and Hurtig (2000), despite mistakenly identifying standpoint theory as simply research coming from women's perspectives, ultimately uphold the contribution standpoint makes to studies of gender in the field of educational anthropology. Fine (2006) offers strong objectivity as a guiding epistemological frame for critical scholarly research, and Sleeter (2000–2001), in her review of research on teacher education and equity, explicitly equates standpoint theory with what she refers to as "emancipatory research" (p. 235).

In addition, while standpoint theory is addressed in synoptic texts on educational research, a handful of specific research projects have made active use of it. For instance, Henry (1996), framing standpoint as "an act of political consciousness" (p. 364), discusses the role of Black women's "oppositional standpoint" in her analysis of the ways that Black women teachers negotiate the cultural and pedagogic norms of predominantly White educational institutions. Bloom and Erlandson (2003) draw on a similar framework in their own analysis of Black, female school administrators and their struggles for recognition within their school contexts. Yonezawa (2000) also makes use of standpoint theory to understand how parents negotiate and make decisions regarding systems of educational tracking, and Andre-Bechely (2005) applies standpoint theory as one lens for analyzing how parents understand and experience school choice policies differently depending on their social locations. Spatig (2005) uses standpoint theory to critique developmentalist classroom practices that often advocate hands-off pedagogies that can produce inequalities, and Cooper (2005) uses Black feminist standpoint to analyze how working-class African American women make sense of school voucher programs. Takacs (2002), in discussing how he addresses positionality in his social-justice oriented teacher education courses, specifically refers to his use of strong objectivity in order to have both students and himself see beyond their socially-located individual perspectives.

Can I learn from this?

Watkins' (1993) work on "Black Curriculum Orientations" essentially describes a form of African American curricular standpoint. Setting the different approaches to African American education within the context of racism in the United States, he explains that:

> Black curriculum theorizing … is inextricably tied to the history of the Black experience in the United States. Black social, political, and intellectual development in all cases evolved under socially oppressive and politically repressive circumstance involving physical and intellectual duress and tyranny.
>
> *(p. 322)*

Watkins goes onto identify six different Black curriculum orientations:

- Functionalist—which focused on rudimentary skills for social functioning;
- accommodationist—which focused vocational training/manual labor "linked to colonialism, segregation, and subservience" (p. 325);
- liberal—consisting of missionary and corporate influenced standard, liberal academics, reconstructionist—which critiqued capitalism as the "facilitator and generator of racism" (p. 332);
- Afrocentrist—which placed the reclamation of traditional African culture at the center of curriculum and pedagogy;
- Black nationalist—which adopted a Pan Africanist, cultural nationalist, and Black separatist focus for learning.

what is this?

What is the difference?

Kumashiro (2002), without naming it as such, essentially applies standpoint in what he frames as "antioppressive education," which he states is:

> not something that happens when the curriculum is no longer partial. Rather, it happens when critical questions … are being asked about the partial curriculum. It is not a curriculum that is fully inclusive or that centers on critical texts. Rather, it is a process of looking beyond the curriculum. It is a process of troubling the official knowledge in the disciplines. It is a process of explicitly trying to read against common sense.
>
> *(p. 62)*

corporate sense that is normalized & made common

Here Kumashiro is suggesting a form of curricular standpoint, one that actively challenges commonsense understandings of the world by doing what he terms as, "troubling the official knowledge in the disciplines." Kumashiro thus not only asserts that power relations exist within the structure of our curricular knowledge, but also that antioppressive education, like a standpoint, is something that is achieved through critical analysis (the act of which is itself a form of intellectual action).

Connell's (1994) work is one of the few that takes up standpoint theory within curriculum studies specifically. Connell's concept of "curricular justice" suggests that, if schools are to work for social justice, then they must examine the world from the "standpoint of the least advantaged" (p. 43), where:

> The "standpoint of the least advantaged" means, concretely, that we think through economic issues from the standpoint of the poor, not the rich. We think through gender arrangements from the standpoint of women. We think through race relations and land questions from the standpoint of indigenous people. We think through questions of sexuality from the standpoint of gay people. And so on.
>
> (p. 43)

Connell thus advocates that curriculum take the standpoint of the marginalized or oppressed because, "the current hegemonic curriculum embodies the interests of the *most* advantaged. Justice requires a *counter*-hegemonic curriculum … designed to embody the interests and perspectives of the least advantaged" (p. 44, original emphasis). Hence we see Connell taking up the cardinal basis for standpoint—that curricular knowledge is intimately connected to power relations in society, and that such relations are thus transmitted within hegemonic knowledge projects, including in schools. It is important to note that ample research supports Connell's argument as it applies to school curriculum (see, e.g., Au, 2009f; Au & Apple, 2009a; C. Sleeter & J. Stillman, 2005).

Of all the educational research and theorizing discussed here, DeLissovoy (2008) offers the most developed treatment of standpoint theory. In his analysis of conceptions of oppression in educational theory, DeLissovoy correctly traces the lineage of standpoint theory from Marx to the Marxist philosopher Georg Lukacs (1971) to Hartsock (1983), whom he says, "transposes the notion of class position in Marxism onto the category of gender in arguing for a feminist political and epistemological standpoint" (DeLissovoy, 2008, p. 84). While highlighting the political-philosophical strength of this epistemological turn, DeLissovoy (2008) then goes on to discuss what he sees as the limitations of Hartsock's (1983) and others' (e.g., Collins, 2000; Harding, 1997) conceptions of standpoint theory, mainly that if we take each distinct social position as the basis for a standpoint, then, "each standpoint ultimately appears inadequate for understanding social life outside of the characteristic experience of that group" (DeLissovoy, 2008, p. 85).

Other educational researchers have also made sharp and sometimes erroneous critiques of standpoint theory. One such line of critiques represents positivist attacks on epistemologies and methodologies that take context and subjectivity into account. For instance, some scholars ultimately seek to deny the contextual basis for all knowledge while simultaneously denying the existence of hierarchies of power that determine social location (see, e.g., Landau, 2008) and hence have incorrectly labeled standpoint theory as a "wholly discredited theory of science" (Pinnick, 2008, p. 1056). Other lines of critique represent misunderstandings and misconstructions of standpoint theory itself. Siegel (2006), for instance, misconstrues epistemological standpoints as perspectives that simply arise from essentialist, universal positionalities associated with identity politics—a position that explicitly contradicts both Hartsock's (1998a) and Harding's (2004a, 2004b) conception of standpoint, outlined above. In his critique of standpoint theory Siegel (2006) goes on to conflate neutrality with strong objectivity, and then argues for the lack of neutrality in all research. Siegel's critique proves ironic because not only is it factually incorrect since Harding's (2004b) notion of strong objectivity is foundationally based on the idea that there is no neutrality at all, but Siegel (2006) then goes on to uphold the very kind of subjectivity that Harding (2004b) herself advocates for quite clearly in her analysis.

These positivistic and erroneous attacks aside, there are some critical issues to address with how standpoint theory has been used in educational research. Henry (1996), Andre-Bechely (2005), and Foley et al. (2000) for instance, despite their constructive use of standpoint theory, incorrectly frame it as mainly a feminist project that only takes women's perspectives into account. Indeed, this applies to DeLissovoy's (2008) explanation of standpoint theory as well, despite his quite powerful analysis. In my read of Hartsock (1998a), especially her more recent writings, I do not see her arguing for a standpoint epistemology that only applies to a singular social group (e.g., women only, as part of a feminist standpoint), as DeLissovoy (2008) specifically outlines in his critique. Rather, as explained in my above detailing of her work, for Hartsock (1998a) the issue is that of the standpoint of the oppressed, with an explicit recognition of how gender, in combination with other social locations such as race, class, and sexuality, influences how we "know" the world, which in turn influences and informs all research/knowledge projects in some way. As such, educational researchers making use of standpoint theory to look at intersections of gender and race (Andre-Bechely, 2005; Bloom & Erlandson, 2003; Henry, 1996), for instance, could further strengthen their analyses by explicitly acknowledging how class, race, sexuality and other aspects of our identities are an integral part of standpoint theory as well (Harding, 2004b).

Further, it is important to note that my own critique of DeLissovoy (2008) here is friendly and constructive, as his work has pushed on the edges of critical educational research in very positive ways, and his considerations of standpoint theory in educational research remain some of the most theoretically and conceptually developed. Indeed, in this case, it seems to me that DeLissovoy's work would simply benefit from a reading of Hartsock's (1998a, 1998b) more recent writings, which include

---

Handwritten margin notes:

Au: Apple wrote: critical educational theory
Ladson-Billings et al: critical race educational theory
↳ Culturally-Responsive Pedagogy
↠ focuses only on Black stu in Black Schools. While teaches don't know how to teach about Black issues to white students

Excellent point in attack in Siegel.

Au is a sweetheart ♡ Love how he uses language to critique & support

specific replies to her critiques and increased clarity in her conception of standpoint theory. Indeed, my engagement with DeLissovoy (2008) points to the most significant critique to be made of how standpoint theory has been used in educational theory generally, and curriculum studies more specifically: It has been under-theorized. This is critical because, if standpoint theory is to be used more widely in education and fields such as curriculum studies, then a more fully elaborated framework is required. In what follows I offer such a framework in hopes that it can exist as a tool for the revitalization of curriculum studies, one that both acknowledges relations of power in school knowledge, but one that also is committed to the reformation of those same relations as they exist concretely in schools and society.

Standpoint Theory and Progressive Education

One impetus for my attempt to bring standpoint theory more concretely into education, as well as offer a more elaborately articulated conception of standpoint theory for educational research, is that I'm not sure that our arguments for many progressive curricular projects, be they framed in terms of social justice, antioppressive, critical, multicultural, anti-bias, etc., are strong enough for the struggles against the rightward turn of curricular politics in this country and around the world (Apple, 2006; Au & Apple, 2009a). While all of these orientations are crucial to the overall struggle about the politics of school knowledge and the curriculum, I do not think that we (and as a critical scholar and education activist, I count myself amongst this "we") articulate a strong enough argument and justification for the importance of standpoint in our work; that oftentimes we rely on arguments and justifications that are relativistic at best and ineffective at worst. *= all are equal*

For instance, to take the field of multicultural education as a broad example, scholars have argued the value of what loosely amounts to a multicultural standpoint in the curriculum along several lines. Most prominently, it is argued, multicultural education is important because of a moral imperative (see, e.g., Stables, 2005), a demographic imperative linked to the changing racial and cultural makeup of the public school population (see, e.g., Hodgkinson, 2002), a global citizenship imperative regarding the politics of nation-state relative to increasing immigration and international fluctuations of various populations (see, e.g., Banks, 2008, 2009), and a democratic citizenship imperative that, like the demographic imperative, extends from changes in population in the United States, but speaks specifically to the need for a more popular, participatory democracy, one that embraces a much broader portion of the populace (see, e.g., Marri, 2005).

These arguments for multicultural education are all important: They have all been wielded in support of a larger project to make public education more democratic, as well as to develop a better informed student populace in hopes of increasing equality generally. Indeed, all of these positions are significant within our collective struggles against rise of conservatism in school knowledge (Apple, 2006), and the more tools we have at our disposal, the better positioned we are to struggle against the regressive educational politics in the United States and globally. In this manner I support these scholars and the ways that they have positioned themselves within educational research and reform, because, by and large, we are all working on knowledge projects aimed at developing a more just society. Several of the scholars I've used in this example are in fact friends and colleagues whose work I respect very much (see, e.g., Banks, 2008, 2009; Marri, 2005).

However, I believe that the above arguments for multicultural education share one shortcoming: They rely on a politics of relativism. For instance, take the moral imperative for multicultural education discussed above (see, e.g., Stables, 2005). The problem is that morals are fundamentally relative to an individual or individual group's particular perspective. Thus, to argue solely on moral grounds for the importance of multicultural education in our schools and classrooms is to engage in an argument in which no position is necessarily "correct," where all anyone can do is deliberate over particular positions and make a decision based on those arguments. While such a process of deliberation may prove fruitful as an intellectual exercise that promotes critical thinking (Parker, 2005), it also presupposes that all arguments are of equal weight, that the Eurocentric, fundamentally racist arguments against multicultural education (see, e.g., Hirsch, 1996) hold the same value as the anti-racist arguments in support of multicultural education (see, e.g., Vavrus, 2002).

The other imperatives for multicultural education, mentioned above, face a similar difficulty. For instance, the demographic imperative (see, e.g., Hodgkinson, 2002) rests on an assumptive argument that the curriculum of our schools should match our student population, in part, as preparation for dealing with the diversity found within society. While I absolutely agree with this assumption and have actively advocated it myself in my own work in education, it is also an argument that is somewhat weak politically because ultimately it hinges on yet another relativist issue: the question of the role of schools. The problem with the demographic imperative for multicultural education is this: If one sees schools mainly as providing acculturation to a superior and/or dominant Eurocentric culture based on understanding the canon of Western Civilization (see, e.g., Hirsch, 1996), then multicultural education either needs to be shaped to fit within that narrative (Buras, 2008), or it does not fall within the accepted bounds of "official knowledge" (Apple, 2000). Once again we are left defending relative positions of the role of schools and the sanctioned knowledge schools communicate relative to how we define that role. Thus, the demographic imperative leaves no position which can be defended simply because the issue of the role of schools is itself highly contested and leaves room for justification from several perspectives (progressive and conservative alike).

Indeed, the other two imperatives for multicultural education discussed above— global citizenship (see, e.g., Banks, 2008, 2009) and democratic citizenship (see, e.g.,

[handwritten margin note at top: Neoconservatism: born in US in 1960s among liberal hawks who became bothered by increasing pacifist foreign policy of Democratic Party & the development of New Left's & counter culture of the 1960 especially Vietnam protests.]

Marri, 2005)—encounter this same difficulty, because both revolve around the same contested issue regarding the role of schools. What separates these from the other imperatives, however, is that they rely on a political argument surrounding healthier, more vibrant democracies. Such a position, to my mind, provides a much more robust argument for multicultural education, particularly because it draws on commonsense notions of democracy and democratic education (Gutmann, 1990), and such notions are often rhetorically accepted as a commonsense, universal good.

[handwritten margin note: Democracy & Citizenship definitions are contested & shaped by political positions]

However, in addition to being caught within relativist perspectives about the functions of schooling in the United States, the citizenship arguments for multicultural education get further complicated by the struggles of the definitions of democracy and citizenship—concepts which themselves are highly contested and equally relative to specific political positions (Apple, 2004, Ch. 9). Indeed, the contestation over citizenship and how it relates to democracy has only sharpened with the rise of ethno-centric nationalism and xenophobia in the United States (Wise, 2010).

[handwritten margin note: Explanation of how SP is more comprehensive than the other imperatives to justify its use as a framework]

As a challenge to relativism, I would also assert that standpoint provides the strongest argument for the need for multicultural education in our schools because standpoint requires that we engage in arguments about material and social reality. Because standpoint, as discussed above, takes as its basis that the perspectives and life experiences of the marginalized or oppressed provide clearer, more objective understandings of the world, we can use standpoint to wage a particularly robust defense of multicultural education: Using race/culture as one axis of analysis, the perspectives of people of color become central to understanding social and material realities, because it is that standpoint, as peoples whose knowledge is marginalized within the current social, historical, and institutional contexts (Darder & Torres, 2004; McCarthy, 1990), that provides stronger objectivity through their experiences with the racism—a reality which is obscured within dominant and hegemonic perspectives. *[handwritten: to change curriculum.]*

Granted, one can argue whether or not the race conscious standpoint of people of color is valid or invalid simply by arguing about whether or not racism exists. However, standpoint theory can take up (and ultimately "win") this argument because it relies on the epistemological claim that we can look at material and social realities. To this end we could present data regarding peoples' individual and group experiences and testimony regarding individual and collective experiences, and illustrate quite clearly that racial disparities—as evidence of racism—do in fact actually exist (see, e.g., Kidder & Rosner, 2002–3; Ladson-Billings, 2006), particularly when the level of analysis moves beyond just that of only the individual. Consequently, the grounds for argument that arise from standpoint revolve around the actual material and social existence of people. Thus, to deny the existence of racism means to wage an argument that openly contradicts both the anecdotal and qualitative data that arises from the experiences of people of color, as well as the overwhelming amount of quantitative data that exists which demonstrates institutionally based racial inequalities (Wise, 2008). What standpoint then brings to a

[handwritten annotation at top: Neoliberalism: 20th cent resurgence of 19th cen idea of free market Capitalism ⇒ Conservative + libertarian + privatization + deregulation + globalization + free trade + austerity. reduce government spending on social services and ↑ role of private sector.]

defense of multicultural education is the position that, if we want a fuller, more "true" representation of what exists in the world—if we want to actually understand the world as it is—then we must prioritize the perspectives of people of color (and other marginalized groups) in our curriculum (Au, 2009b) and be justified in doing so.

In making the above arguments regarding power and hegemony in curricular knowledge, however, it is critical to recognize that existing curricular knowledge does not only represent that of dominant groups, but also embodies progressive, counter-hegemonic victories small and large (Apple & Christian-Smith, 1991). In many cases the curriculum is a product of what Apple (1988, 2000) calls "curriculum accords," where "elements of the knowledge of a number of classes, class fractions, and social movements are in a sometimes contradictory relation" (Apple, 1988, p. 198). For instance, due to the efforts of the above-mentioned scholars in multicultural education, as well as that of community activists, such accords might include the incorporation of certain types of multiculturalism in textbooks sitting side by side with the traditional Western canon, and be representative of perhaps a partial or incomplete victory for those groups with less power (Apple, 2000). Indeed, much of the curriculum analyzed in Chapter 5 illustrates the fact that progressive curriculum that does not necessarily align with dominant interests exists in many corners. The overall point being, however, that just as knowledge is a site of struggle (one of the fundaments of standpoint theory), so too is the curriculum always a site of struggle. This means that any curriculum is likely to contain both regressive and progressive elements.

[handwritten margin note: curriculum accords contain progressive & regressive elements! Wow!]

Towards a Framework for Curricular Standpoint

In light of the above discussion, I would argue that it is crucial that standpoint theory be brought more substantively and consciously into the curriculum—on both political and epistemological grounds. Politically, standpoint is useful in the struggle over school knowledge because conservative forces continue to advance their cultural and intellectual agendas in education through a variety of means, including neoliberal privatization (Burch, 2009; Hursh, 2000), neoconservative politics (Apple, 2006), and the hegemonic control of knowledge through standards (Sleeter & Stillman, 2005), textbooks (Apple, 2000), and high-stakes testing (Au, 2009f), among others. Any struggle over knowledge, however, is also a struggle over epistemology, a struggle over whose understanding counts and what perspectives and politics that understanding carries with it. Put differently, we must ask the question: Whose perception of reality is considered/constructed as valid or invalid in school knowledge, and why? In this regard, and as I discussed above, standpoint theory and its explicit focus on social location establishes the struggle over social and material reality as the basis for epistemology, and it is this struggle that provides the strongest grounds for progressive, social justice curriculum projects.

Thus, drawing on standpoint theory, I suggest the following as a way to more fully conceive of curricular standpoint:

- First, curricular knowledge, as extension of material and social relations, structures our understanding of the world in ways that is both limiting and enabling. In this sense, the curriculum itself communicates epistemologies associated with particular social locations, and in doing so creates potentialities for understanding material reality more clearly or in more obscurity relative to such locations.

- Second, because schools and school knowledge are embedded in and structured by systems of domination and rule that are organized hierarchically around power relations of race, class, gender, sexuality, nationality, and other forms of socially determined categorical difference, the curricular knowledge asserted by groups in power generally supports status quo, hegemonic social relations and epistemologies. This curricular knowledge thus often contradicts and runs counter to the epistemologies and curricular knowledge advanced by oppressed groups. Put differently, the curriculum of the ruler will in many ways be oppositional to the curriculum of the ruled.

- Third, because of unequal power relations, the curricular perspectives of those in power are made operational in generally hegemonic and commonsense forms in school knowledge for everyone, regardless of social location and regardless of whether or not such perspectives are congruent with or contradict the material and social realities of students and their communities. Put differently, despite progressive curricular gains or curriculum accords made by educators and activists, the unequal distribution of power leads to the unequal distribution of specific curricular knowledge, where those with more power can exert stronger influence on our commonsense understandings of the world vis-à-vis the curriculum, even if such commonsense understandings fundamentally operate as distorted conceptions of material and social reality.

- Fourth, because school knowledge is always embedded within dominant power relations, curricular standpoint is thus always born of struggle against those very same power relations. In this sense, curricular standpoint is achieved, not given, because it arises from active, systematic, and conscious work against the reigning, hegemonic, institutionalized forms of curricular knowledge.

- Fifth, curricular standpoint carries with it the potential for human liberation because it works to reveal unequal social and material relations as part of a process which can (not will) lead to the taking of action to change those same unequal social and material relations. Hence, curricular standpoint helps in the development of "oppositional consciousness" (Sandoval, 2000) as students potentially develop ways of understanding the world that can trigger their own resistance to both status quo knowledge and relations, which in turn develops their capacity to take transformational action both individually and socially. Further, this potentiality within curricular standpoint moves those in power to

what is the difference b/w oppositional and critical consciousness)?

work to undermine and discredit curricular projects that seek to challenge dominant social and material relations. Additionally, curricular standpoint requires that we seek to develop strong objectivity relative to curricular knowledge, that we be strongly reflexive not only about the standpoint of knowledge itself, but also strongly reflexive about the origins, politics, and process of how knowledge itself makes its way into the curriculum. Indeed, curricular standpoint is itself a product of strong objectivity, as it immediately and explicitly recognizes the politics of knowledge in such a way that places the curriculum itself on the same plane as the subject knowledge, classroom relations, and pedagogic discourse that constitute the curriculum.

Curricular Standpoint, Recursively

Before concluding this chapter, and to help make sense of the series of conceptual linkages I am making here, I think it is important to explicitly address how my conception of curricular standpoint recursively relates to other chapters and analyses I've made thus far. As I argued in Chapter 2, because consciousness is essentially produced through human interaction with our environment (Allman, 1999; Marx & Engels, 1978), it is critical to consider both the types of classroom environments our curriculum creates (Au, 2009a; Huebner, 1970) as well as the types of student consciousness said environments potentially foster.

Thus, because being and knowing are dynamically intertwined within the dialectical relationship between consciousness and our environment (Allman, 1999; Freire, 1998), the content of the curriculum should relate to students' contexts, experiences, identities, and material realities if it is to be effective (see, e.g., Ladson-Billings, 1997). Put differently, not relating the curriculum to students effectively alienates their knowing from their being, and turns education into a key factor in producing that alienation. Indeed, this point underscores one of the important reasons for adopting curricular standpoint. Further, because we use tools in the development of consciousness (Vygotsky, 1987), teachers and students should consciously consider what tools they make use of in the curriculum. For the teacher, in this instance, the curriculum itself is a tool that they are using to structure classroom environments that leverage certain forms of consciousness amongst students; for students the actual content of the curriculum (activities, projects, foci of study) is the tool with which they actively engage with their educational/curricular environments.

Additionally, because consciousness is fundamentally social in its development and structure (Leont'ev, 1981; Vygotsky, 1987), it is important to not only recognize that social relations are present in every facet of epistemology (Harding, 2004b; Hartsock, 1998a), curriculum, and instruction vis-à-vis the politics of knowledge of content (Apple, 2000) and classroom interactions (Freire, 1974; Shor & Freire, 1987), but also to recognize that the curriculum needs to be connected to material conditions— another argument for the importance of curricular standpoint. Further still, because

Positivism

Pragmatism

consciousness implies thinking about thinking, volitional action, and intentionality towards the world (Davis & Freire, 1981; Vygotsky, 1987), the curriculum, particularly curricular standpoint, can create the potential for teachers (through their practice) and students (through their learning) to engage in the development of meta-awareness of individual and social relations (Au, 2007c; Lukacs, 1971; Vygotsky, 1987).

Because being critical in our reflection is central to developing consciousness that can challenge existing, unequal social relations and work towards more equitable and just social change (Allman, 2007; Freire, 1974), curricular standpoint seeks to foster systematic understandings of the social, cultural, and material world amongst students in order to establish the conditions for them to develop more complex and complete knowledge of themselves and their contexts (see, e.g., Bigelow, 2006). The development of such consciousness thus opens up the possibility for students to develop new potentials for acting relative to their contexts, which in turn creates potential for students to actively interrupt inequality as change agents working for social justice (Bernstein, 1996).

As an extension of the above points, because our consciousness is expressed through praxis—the dialectically unified process of thinking and doing (Allman, 2007; Freire, 1982a, 1982c), the curriculum is powerful if it is linked to action in some form and thus is a point of curricular standpoint. This implies using pedagogy that actively engages students in learning and it implies that one of the objectives of curriculum is for students to take some form of action (in the present or future) in their own social, cultural, political, and economic contexts (see, e.g., Yang & Duncan-Andrade, 2005)—with the caveat that learning is itself a form of action taken at the individual level. Indeed, the curriculum can only develop and maintain critical consciousness when teachers, students, and communities recognize that they actually have the power to do so (Counts, 1932).

Conclusion

In this chapter I have pushed into new territory within curriculum studies by advancing a theory of and justification for curricular standpoint. In bringing the work of feminist standpoint theorists into education, I have sought to do two things generally. First, I've suggested an epistemologically strong argument for the justification of standpoint, and by extension social justice, in our curricular practices. Second, and of conceptual importance, feminist standpoint theory, as well as the framework for curricular standpoint I've outlined here, effectively addresses the positivistic/pragmatic and the subjective/postmodern paradigmatic split within curriculum studies discussed in Chapter 1. Standpoint theory both recognizes the subjectivity of socially situated human knowledge about the world and recognizes the importance of addressing material relations and issues. In this way standpoint theory effectively reconciles the tension that exists between the politics of recognition (identity) and the politics of redistribution (material/structural) discussed by Fraser (1995), who offers that:

[T]his distinction between economic injustice and cultural injustice is analytical. In practice, the two are intertwined. Even the most material economic institutions have a constitutive, irreducible cultural dimension; they are shot through with significations and norms. Conversely, even the most discursive cultural practices have a constitutive, irreducible political-economic dimension; they are underpinned by material supports. Thus, far from occupying two airtight separate spheres, economic injustice and cultural injustice are usually interimbricated so as to reinforce one another dialectically. Cultural norms that are unfairly biased against some are institutionalized in the state and the economy; meanwhile, economic disadvantage impedes equal participation in the making of culture, in public spheres and in everyday life.

intertwined   *hinders*   *(pp. 72–73)*

As such, curriculum studies would benefit from standpoint theory because it provides a conceptual and political synthesis that attends to culture/identity and to issues of materiality and practice.

Curricular standpoint, as I've conceptualized it here, offers an even more powerful tool for justifying the privileging of marginalized or oppressed groups in our curricula—an appeal to understanding material and social reality as it exists in ways that are more truthful and more objective than what hegemonic perspectives provide us. If we want students to understand the world more fully, then we have to offer a curricular standpoint that surfaces the issues of peoples and communities that are either regularly pushed to the margins of school knowledge, actively misconstrued within the curriculum, or left out of the curriculum completely. Thus the conception of curricular standpoint I've offered here not only contributes to the growth of critical educational theory, but also provides classroom teachers who teach for social justice with curricular logics that they can use to justify the choices they make in their practices.

However, in bringing standpoint theory more deeply into education generally and curriculum studies specifically, I do want to reiterate an important point, one that serves as a caution against an important and common misunderstanding of standpoint generally: Social location, within the context of socio-economic relations, is what determines standpoint. Thus, we cannot simply fragment standpoint to constitute all the various subjectivities we might find in any given society, if for no other reason than unequal power relations are hegemonic, and standpoint arises from the social location of the marginalized or oppressed. Standpoint does not simply equal perspective in the colloquial sense that "everybody has a standpoint." Rather, standpoint refers to the socially situated perspective of the oppressed or marginalized.

Further, it is critical to highlight that standpoint is considered a *starting point* for knowledge projects—as epistemological and methodological grounds for inquiry into understanding the world. As such, it shapes the kinds of questions we ask and the overall orientation of our knowledge projects and our curriculum. In this sense, Connell's (1994) treatment of standpoint in social justice education is precisely right:

If we want to understand patriarchy and sexism, then, given the power and privilege of men in our current social relations, we stand a better chance of getting a clearer, more strongly objective understanding of patriarchy and sexism if we take up the standpoint of women. This immediately implies two things relative to my discussion in this chapter. First, it means that standpoints should not automatically be fragmented abstractly into the various possible subjectivities that simply exist in our world. To do so would incorrectly give rise to the idea that different standpoints somehow compete with each other for being closer to material reality. Rather, standpoints exist relative to specific knowledge projects, as part of specific inquiries into specific phenomena, all of which exist within specific social relations. What this means is that we are never taking up standpoint in the general sense and instead must always be looking at standpoint in reflexive relation to the specific object, process, or area of study. Second, it means that standpoint in the curriculum (as well as in the study of curriculum) functions relative to the specific social, political, and economic context of schools and school knowledge. This final point, as well as what it means to put curricular standpoint into practice, will be illustrated by the concrete examples offered in Chapter 5.

5

CURRICULUM OF THE OPPRESSED: CURRICULAR STANDPOINT IN PRACTICE

In the previous chapter I provided a detailed treatment of standpoint theory, its use (and misuse) in educational research, and attempted to reframe standpoint as both a method of inquiry into curriculum, as well as a justification for contextualizing the content of the curriculum within our socio-economic, cultural, and political realities. In this chapter I illustrate curricular standpoint in both form and function by looking at some historical examples of curricular standpoint that specifically take up counter-hegemonic politics relative to their times, and then I offer an analysis of contemporary curriculum across several subject areas.

Before continuing, however, I would like to take a moment to summarize the basic framework for curricular standpoint I developed in the previous chapter, as this framework guides the analysis done here.

① Lesson as it is what does it enable? What does it limit?

- Curricular knowledge, as extension of material and social relations, structures our understanding of the world in ways that is both limiting and enabling.
- Curricular knowledge asserted by groups in power generally supports status quo, hegemonic social relations, and epistemologies such that the curriculum of the ruler will in many ways be oppositional to the curriculum of the ruled.
- Despite progressive gains in some areas of the curriculum, the curricular perspectives of those in power are made operational in generally hegemonic and *dominating* commonsense forms in school knowledge for everyone. *If comercial lesson what power*
- Curricular standpoint is achieved, not given, because it arises from active, sys- *structures are reflected in the* tematic, and conscious work against the reigning, hegemonic, institutionalized *lesson?* forms of curricular knowledge.
- Curricular standpoint carries with it the potential for human liberation because it works to reveal unequal social and material relations as part of a process which can (not will) lead to the taking of action to change those same unequal social and material relations.

- Curricular standpoint is itself a product of strong objectivity, as it immediately and explicitly recognizes the politics of knowledge in such a way that places the curriculum itself (as an object) on the same plane as the subject knowledge contained within the curriculum.

Curricular Standpoint Historically

Examples of curricular standpoint exist historically, but, because of their counter-hegemonic politics, they have often been relegated to the margins of educational history. In this section I offer examples of individuals and groups that illustrate curricular standpoint in practice historically. I then follow these exemplars with some more contemporary examples. In all cases my intent is to look at how curricular standpoint manifests concretely in policy and practice, as well as attempt to carry forward the methodological and epistemological commitments of standpoint as a guide for my analysis.

Socialist Sunday Schools

One historical example of curricular standpoint can be found in the Socialist Sunday schools. Between 1909 and 1911, over 100 Socialist school officials were elected to various school districts across the United States (Teitelbaum, 1988). As Teitelbaum (1988) explains:

> Radical educational critics of the time were becoming more aware that working-class viewpoints were being systematically eliminated from public schools when they stood in opposition to dominant capitalist interests. The political slant of school curriculum was hardly sympathetic to the forces of reform, let alone radical change, in American society.
>
> *(p. 35)*

Socialist critics also found that public schools were teaching students to embrace profit and greed as well as accept social conditions like poverty (Teitelbaum, 1988).

The Socialist critiques were supported by empirical research as well. In 1922, George S. Counts published a major study of four U.S. cities and found that these systems of education mainly served only the most privileged parts of the population and ran counter to the American Democratic ideal. He came to similar conclusions in a later study of 1,654 school boards across the United States (Counts, 1927/ 1969). While Counts was not Socialist, he did see democracy as a measure of control over the inequalities created by capitalist profit-making (Kliebard, 2004). In response to these conditions, between 1900 and 1920, Socialist activists established more than 100 English-speaking Sunday schools in 20 states, ranging in size from classes of 10 students to schools that enrolled more than 600 students (Teitelbaum, 1988). The curricula of these schools emphasized that: (1) Children should take pride in being working class; (2) Workers are systematically subordinated and should find solidarity with other oppressed groups; (3) Students should develop a sense of collectivism; (4) Students learned about the connections of their immediate social conditions with the broader socio-economic relations; (5) Fundamental social change is absolutely necessary; and (6) The contemporary socio-economic relations needed to be critically analyzed in light of commonsense understandings of the world (Teitelbaum, 1991).

These Socialist Sunday schools represent a form of curricular standpoint in practice. First, they recognized that curricular knowledge structures our understanding of the world, and thus were concerned with how the politics of hegemonic capitalist curriculum limited and enabled certain forms of consciousness. In this sense the Socialist Sunday schools knew fundamentally that the curriculum of the owners would in most ways be oppositional to a curriculum of the workers. Additionally, with their curricular focus on workers rights, collectivity, understanding socio-economic relations, and emphasizing social change, the Socialist Sunday schools offered a proletarian/working class curricular standpoint that challenged the hegemonic socio-economic relations and ideology of the time, making their curricular standpoint an achievement against norms. As such, the Socialist Sunday schools' curriculum carried the potential for human liberation in that it sought to advance epistemologies that resisted the status quo relations and enable students to develop forms of consciousness that fostered collective action against mass exploitation. In these ways we could say that the Socialist Sunday schools developed a curriculum that structured educational environments such that students could access counter hegemonic forms of anti-capitalist knowledge, with the hopes that such knowledge would develop forms of critical consciousness.

The Work of Carter G. Woodson

The lifework of Carter G. Woodson is another historical example of curricular standpoint in practice. Born in 1875, Carter G. Woodson earned his doctorate from Harvard in 1912, becoming the only person in U.S. history with slave parentage to earn a Ph.D. (Dagbovie, 2004). As an African American scholar, educator, and activist, Woodson was concerned about the *Mis-Education of the Negro* (Woodson, 1990/ 1933), given the Eurocentric and overtly racist historical knowledge that African American children and adults were learning in schools at the time (Dagbovie, 2004; King, Crowley, & Brown, 2010; Levine, 2000). Such racist mis-education, Woodson argued, meant that African Americans knew " 'practically nothing' about their history and that without this knowledge 'the race' could become 'a negligible factor in the thought of the world' and stood 'in danger of being exterminated' ..." (Woodson, as quoted in Dagbovie, 2004, p. 375). Thus, as King et al. (2010) explain:

> [F]or Woodson, the retelling of African history was not simply to challenge the historical canon or just to document ancient histories, but also to show

that people of African descent were not just enslaved, colonized, or primitive people—but a people of profound literary, scientific, and intellectual accomplishments. Thus, Woodson's efforts at retelling African history were at the forefront of his overarching philosophical and political project of challenging and reconstructing academic and school knowledge about Africans in America.

(p. 213)

As such, Woodson became a powerful advocate for the development of a curriculum that, in the context of racist schooling within a racist society, took up the standpoint of African Americans as vital contributors to the cultural and intellectual history of the world.

Woodson was as prolific as he was driven in his fight against racism. The founder of *Negro History Week* (which later became *Black History Month*), Woodson founded and edited both *The Journal of Negro History* (now *The Journal of Black History*) and *The Negro History Bulletin*, wrote or edited 20 books relevant to the history and culture of Africa and African Americans, and developed educational resources aimed specifically at students, teachers, and the general public (Dagbovie, 2007; King et al., 2010).

The development of textbooks, for instance, was one way that Woodson sought to fight against the hegemony of White, racist knowledge of the time. As such, he authored or co-authored several textbooks that openly challenged scientific racism, highlighted the achievements of Africans and African Americans, challenged the racist narrative that African Americans were without a cultural and political history, reconstructed a more true image of Africa and its importance to Black culture, and emphasized slave resistance and rebellion (Brown, 2010). As Levine (2000) explains regarding Woodson and Wesley's (1959/1933) textbook, *The Story of the Negro Retold*:

> In this work Woodson and Wesley counter anti-black myths through describing the civilizations of ancient Africa, notable slave rebellions, and the accomplishments of Reconstruction governments ... They chronicle such little known aspects of American history as the alliance between Indians and blacks during the Seminole Wars ...
>
> *(Levine, 2000, p. 9)*

In addition to recouping African American history, knowledge, and culture through the use of words, Woodson's texts also used photographs of African Americans, "working in diverse settings and contributing new knowledge and innovations to every aspect of the cultural, political, and economic contexts of the United States and abroad" (Brown, 2010, p. 59) as a means to fight the racist images of African Americans so often portrayed in mainstream textbooks and media. As Brown (2010) cogently sums up regarding Woodson's textbooks:

The narratives found in the textbooks sought to fashion an image of the African American that illustrated social progress and competent mental capability. These textbooks clearly served as a counternarrative to the existing racial imagery found during this time in K-12 texts and academic discourse. In addition, the images demonstrated the diversity of African American public life beyond the existing tropes of inferiority and minstrelsy that dominated this historic period. Woodson and Wesley's textbooks were not simplistic, revisionist curriculum making, but examples of a complex, methodological approach of selecting texts and images with the sole purpose of challenging existing discourses of race ...

(p. 60)

Another central part of Carter G. Woodson's curricular project was the publication of the *Negro History Bulletin* (*NHB*). First published in 1937, the *NHB* was written in popular and accessible language. Further, the *NHB* provided a space for African American curricular standpoint to thrive, as Dagbovie (2004) explains,

The *NHB* also served as a dynamic discussion forum for teachers pertaining to curriculum development, politics, black history, and teaching. In a sense, the pages of the *NHB* belonged to black school teachers, serving as their autonomous space for generating epistemologies of black history.

(p. 379)

Thus, the *NHB* served as a supplemental resource for African American teachers who were not only mis-educated about Black history themselves, but who also wanted to teach a more accurate and empowering understanding of African and African American history and culture to schoolchildren (Dagbovie, 2004; King et al., 2010).

Carter G. Woodson's work clearly exhibited aspects of curricular standpoint. First, he saw that the curriculum being taught African Americans was literally limiting their identities and potentials to be powerful, culturally centered people. Fundamentally Woodson thus recognized that the curriculum of the ruler—in this case, the hegemony of White supremacy—was ill-serving African Americans. Thus his entire scholarly and educational project was an achievement against much of the institutionalized curricular knowledge as he actively worked to develop an epistemological resistance to the racist, hegemonic, Eurocentric curriculum of the times. Specifically as such, he himself undertook, as he advocated for others as well, a process of systematic and conscious work against the reigning forms of curricular knowledge—using his scholarly publications as both a platform and a forum to foster African American knowledge and viewpoints on the content of education for Black children. Further, Woodson's entire project was based on the idea that such a curricular standpoint created the potential for African Americans (and allies) to overcome racism on both an individual and institutional level, and thus carried with it the potential for liberatory action for African Americans (and others) to make personal and educational change. In these ways, the curricular work of Carter G. Woodson functionally sought to develop curricular environments where learners (in this case, students and teachers alike) could access non-Eurocentric, anti-racist, African-centric knowledge with the overall goal of developing positive Black identity and critical consciousness.

Virginia Elementary Schools' Course of Study

Another historical example of curricular standpoint can be found in the *Course of Study for Virginia Elementary Schools: Grades I–VII* (Virginia State Board of Education, 1943), published during the sharply unequal Jim Crow era in the U.S. South. These recommendations amounted to a curriculum framework sanctioned by the State of Virginia, and are remarkable for both the process of their production and for their content. In terms of process, the "Acknowledgment" section explained that during the 1940–41 school year, more than 7,000 teachers made suggestions for the content of the *Course of Study*. Based on the suggestions of those 7,000 teachers,

> two groups, one white and one Negro, composed of superintendents, high and elementary principals, elementary supervisors, and elementary teachers met with members of the staff of the State Department of Education for a five weeks' conference which was devoted to the preparation of mimeographed materials to be distributed over the State during the school session of 1941–42.
> *(Virginia State Board of Education, 1943, p. 9)*

The "Acknowledgment" section went on to briefly explain the process this group went through to essentially revise the original input of the 7,000-plus teachers into the *Course of Study*.

The second, and equally notable aspect of the *Course of Study* (Virginia State Board of Education, 1943) is the content of its curricular guidelines, which at times were quite subversive in their stated opposition to social control and inequities associated with capitalism. For instance the *Course of Study* contained subsections that critiqued the elite's use of propaganda and the use of religion for social control, while embracing the idea that the social order can be changed by human intervention. Perhaps where the *Course of Study* gets the most radical is in its suggestions regarding capitalism, wealth, and their relationship with democracy. In the subsection entitled, "The Understanding that Government in a Democracy Is Often Controlled by Forces Invisible to the Citizen," it suggested teaching that:

> Minorities, organized for advancing all types of selfish interests, attempt to control the government, but those with the greatest financial resources have the advantage ...

Powerful minorities secure control of the government in their special interests by subsidizing political parties, investing in propaganda, and by controlling officials of the school, church, and press.

(pp. 551–52)

"Minorities" here, of course, literally referred to numerically small groups of elites, not non-Whites as the term is commonly used to refer to in contemporary times. Later, in a subsection dealing specifically with "Modern Business and Industrial Enterprise," the *Course of Study* recommended teaching that:

The material prosperity of the modern world has been attained under the capitalistic system.

Capitalism is based upon the principle of profit to the owner rather than service to the masses of people.

The methods of distribution of goods in a capitalistic society tend to direct social products into the hands of the few.

Production is based upon the amount of goods purchasers can be induced to consume, rather than upon their needs.

The capitalistic system is not planned and lacks direction; thus waste and economic cycles result.

Natural resources are exploited for profit.

The dependence of the laborer upon capital tends to reduce him to a servile status.

(p. 513)

Other sections dealt with the environmental factors in the development of human culture and civilization (a radical idea that cut against popular genetic explanations of human development of the time) and asserted that capitalism and imperialism have failed to stop wars.

If we think about the State of Virginia *Course of Study* (Virginia State Board of Education, 1943) within the framework of curricular standpoint, we can see that it embodied several key aspects. The first and most obvious is that the process of developing the *Course of Study* included both African American and White teachers in some kind of conjoined procedure. The inclusion of African Americans was particularly remarkable because the development of the *Course of Study* took place in the Jim Crow South. Hence we must assume that the "two groups, one white and one Negro" (p. 9) met separately, in separate facilities, with separate leadership and organization. Although we absolutely cannot assume that the *Course of Study* actually incorporated the input of the "Negro" participants, the possibility does concretely exist that African American educators did have input into this curriculum framework. If it was the case that the *Course of Study* represented the collaborative vision of both White and African American educators, then on one level, this document cut against the hegemonic racial politics relative to the construction of knowledge at the time—especially considering that it took place in the White supremacist South. After all, under Jim Crow in the South, there was no particular need for Whites to bother including African Americans in their curriculum planning except out of some sense of political commitment. Thus the *Course of Study* not only represented a conscious and systematic achievement against institutionalized forms of knowledge, it also potentially recognized African American epistemologies as important and valid within the system of education.

In addition to its racial politics, the *Course of Study* (Virginia State Board of Education, 1943) also illustrates other aspects of curricular standpoint. It is clear from the standards and its description of elites, capitalism, and power, that the *Course of Study* embraced the standpoint of the worker and/or the masses of people—a standpoint that only existed relative to the unequal power relations (and extreme poverty) of the times. In recognizing these power relations, the *Course of Study* essentially acted as an intervention into those very same power relations, since the goal was to educate children according to these standards—thus illustrating it as a curricular achievement that carried with it the potential for liberation. Indeed, the level of this achievement is difficult to fathom relative to our currently conservative social and political context (Apple, 2006), especially given that these were state level standards. Further, in its supremely blunt description of capitalism, the *Course of Study* seemingly recognized the epistemological hegemony of powerful elites, essentially fostering what we might call an "epistemology of the oppressed" (Au, 2007a). In these ways the *Course of Study* sought to create educational environments that potentially allowed African American and White students to access forms of knowledge that specifically developed their class consciousness.

Contemporary Curricular Standpoint

Although they are not explicitly articulated as such, there already exists a number of lesson plan collections and curricula that take up curricular standpoint. These include books such as *Beyond Heroes and Holidays* (Lee, Menkhart, & Okazawa-Rey, 1998), *Putting the Movement Back into Civil Rights Teaching* (Menkhart, Murray, & View, 2004), *Resistance in Paradise* (Wei & Kamel, 1998), and every publication offered by *Rethinking Schools* (see, e.g., Au, Bigelow, & Karp, 2007; Bigelow, 2006; Christensen, 2009b), among others. In what follows I offer some examples of curricular standpoint in contemporary practice in the four dominant school academic subjects of language arts/English, science, mathematics, and social studies.

Language Arts/English Education

Christensen's (2009a), "Putting Out the Linguistic Welcome Mat," provides a brief, concrete example of curricular standpoint in practice in the language arts classroom. In this piece, Christensen discusses her curriculum on language and power and includes classroom strategies and resources she uses with her high school language arts students. Christensen explains:

> During 30 years as a language arts classroom teacher, I realized that if I wanted my students to open up in their writing, to take risks and engage in intellectually demanding work, I needed to challenge assumptions about the superiority of Standard English and the inferiority of the home language of many of my black students: African American Vernacular English, or Ebonics. When students feel attacked by the red pen or the tongue for the way they write or speak, they either make themselves small—turning in short papers— or don't turn papers in at all. To build an engaging classroom where students from different backgrounds felt safe enough to dare to be big and bold in their writing, I had to build a curricular platform for them to stand on. ... I finally realized that I needed to create a curriculum on language and power that examined the roots of language supremacy and analyzed how schools perpetuate the myths of the inferiority of some languages.
>
> *(p. 91)*

Using a variety of films, readings, and writing activities, Christensen introduces her students to the origins and grammatical rules of African American Vernacular English (AAVE), and with stunning effect. She recounts that, as her African American students learned that AAVE actually had systemic linguistic roots in West African culture, they actively began to challenge forms of internalized racism they had taken in relative to their home languages. Further, Christensen highlights how this curriculum aided students in the development of a meta-cognitive understanding of not only the structures of AAVE, but also the relationship between AAVE and Standard English—and thus created the potential for these students to take conscious action relative to their own educational futures through an applied awareness of linguistic tools such as code switching.

Christensen's (2009a) classroom practice clearly takes up curricular standpoint: She explicitly acknowledges the ways in which social relations and systems of domination exist within classroom knowledge and linguistic practice (in this case, AAVE). In an attempt to have her curriculum reflect the social and material realities of her African American students, and in an embrace of the ways in which language intertwines with culture and identity, Christensen's curriculum thus takes up the standpoint of a marginalized form of the English language, and thus also takes up the standpoint of a marginalized racial/cultural group within the United States. In the process she works with students to uncover linguistic relationships that may have been previously obscured from student consciousness. Further, Christensen's curricular standpoint represents a conscious act on the teacher's part, something that, after having reflected on 30 years of teaching, she had to work to achieve in her practice, particularly given the hegemonic role that Standard English plays in cultural and linguistic oppression (Lippi-Green, 2011; Ngugi, 1986). Additionally, we see that this curricular standpoint is also about action in that Christensen (2009a) also sees her curriculum as providing her students with increased abilities to develop their writing skills—a pedagogic move requires action on both the part of the teacher and the students. Finally, although Christensen uses AAVE as her starting point, she is quick to point out that the resources she uses actually speak to a wide range of non-standard forms of the English language. Thus, the issue for Christensen is the validation of "home language," regardless of the cultural specifics of one's home.

Science Education

An example of curricular standpoint in science education can be found in the work of Dean (2007), who taught a unit on global warming to her class of predominantly White, working and middle class students in a middle school science class. As Dean explains,

> In the unit I taught, I wanted my students to understand the physics and chemistry that explain the anthropogenic (human-produced) causes of climate change. I also hoped my students would reflect on their own lives and consider how their own behavior could change to become more "climate friendly."
>
> *(pp. 57–58)*

However, when Dean first began the unit she encountered significant resistance. Like so many others in the United States, her students were highly dependent on driving in most aspects of their lives, and regionally, as Dean quips, "I teach in truck country" (p. 58)—a statement that points to the rural, White, and working class cultural milieu of her students. Thus, when Dean began to raise issues associated with car emissions and greenhouse gases, students took umbrage and asked her, "Ms. Dean, are you trying to tell me I can't drive a truck?" (p. 57). Additionally, many of the students in Dean's classes lived too far from school to walk or ride a bike, so they couldn't see any feasible alternatives to driving, causing one student to angrily remark, "I don't get it. What are going to do? Stop driving?" (p. 59). Such resistance caused Dean to ask herself, "How could I teach about the fossil fuel causes of global warming and at the same time respect local identity?" (p. 59).

Knowing that students' lives were deeply connected to driving (and I would argue that their connection to driving was also an expression of their social location), Dean (2007) proceeded to work through a curriculum unit that explored the scientifically proven signs of rising temperatures, including shrinking polar sea ice, permafrost melts, rising water levels in the Marshall Islands, and the vectors of tropical diseases (which are affected by flooding and shifts in extreme weather patterns). Dean also spent time teaching the scientific principles at work, including demonstrations that illustrated how water expands when it is heated, how air and water convection currents work, and how the greenhouse effect worked when gases trapped heat.

After students were able to develop a strong enough science background, Dean (2007) then drew on their personal experiences by asking students to develop lengthy flow charts of what it took to produce something of their choosing. For instance, as Dean explains, some students examined an aluminum can, finding out that it took electricity to produce aluminum, which in turn required a dam or some other power plant to produce electricity, which in turn needed concrete to construct the power plant, which in turn needed mined rock to make concrete, which in turn required an excavator to mine the rock. When a student asked about what it took to produce an excavator, Dean directed her to ask a classroom peer, one who was familiar with large construction machines because of family experience. This same group then started to chart what it took to produce the road needed to drive the excavator to the mines, as well as the different metals, fluids, and oil needed to build and run the excavator. Dean then offered a mini-lecture on the anthropogenic sources of common greenhouse gases (e.g., deforestation, hydropower, livestock digestion, the extraction and production of fossil fuels, landfills, and fossil-fuel combustion), and asked students to brainstorm a list of every use of fossil fuel they could come up with. As Dean remarks, "By the end of the period they saw greenhouse gases everywhere—in tailpipes of tractors, in stockyards, in the power behind the pump, in oil wells, in the manufacturing of hydraulic fluid, in the coal that powered the cement kiln" (p. 61). Finally, after a performance assessment of student knowledge of greenhouse gas production, Dean asked students what kind of action (if any) they might want to take to combat global warming. Through delib-eration, students chose the development of a recycling program at their school. Thus, despite some initial reservations that such a program was simplistic because it doesn't necessarily challenge the roots of consumption, Dean worked with students to under-stand how recycling can result in the reduction of some greenhouse gas production.

Dean's (2007) curriculum on global warming demonstrates curricular standpoint in some key and interesting ways. Most obvious is the choice of topic. While dealing with issues of driving, fossil-fuel consumption/combustion, and greenhouse gases connect to everyone's life in some way, these topics are particularly close to the social location of Dean's students (White, rural, and working/middle class). Thus, because she teaches in "truck country," Dean's choice of topic invites the standpoint of her students in the curriculum (literally creating an educational environment that makes the knowledge more accessible). Dean's curricular standpoint also implicitly recognizes the politics of scientific knowledge, and also illustrated an achievement, as she and her students struggled to overcome hegemonic, more commonsense (and certainly less scientific) forms of knowledge about greenhouse gases and global warming. Further, even though it was quite limited in scope, ambition, and critical consciousness, the recycling project that Dean's students undertook does represent a form of action that holds the potential for larger transformations (and, perhaps, forms of liberation as well should students continue to make meta-connections between their lives and the cultural, economic, social, and political systems that are so reliant on fossil fuels and the destruction of the environment).

However, what I think is the more critically interesting and important point to be found in Dean's curricular standpoint is the way in which she engages her students' social location. By taking up the anthropogenic sources for global warming, Dean engaged the standpoint of her students' social location through their resistance: Given their White, working/middle class backgrounds and cultural/regional connections to trucking (as well as an historical economic reliance on the logging industry), she knew from the start to expect student resistance. Their socially located standpoint nearly guaranteed it. In this interesting, dialectically "negative" or contradictory way, Dean took up a form of curricular standpoint with her students. As Dean reflects, "The student resistance that resulted may have cost us valuable learning and time. On the other hand, that activated resistance may have created in my students a powerful need to know that kept them engaged until we decided on action" (p. 62). The socially located standpoint of her students contributed to their resistance, and Dean made use of this resistance, of their social location, to start a knowledge project about the relationship between climate change and fossil fuels. Eventually, after developing enough scientific knowledge of material reality to work through their resistance, students demonstrated a much more critical consciousness about the relationship between driving, fossil-fuel production/combustion, and global warming. Indeed, this point is critical, because I think it illustrates how curricular standpoint can be used to engage the epistemological resistance of learners, particularly when such resistance is based on consciousness about something (like global warming) that might be incomplete and shaped in ways more congruent with hegemonic ideology—and contradictory to material reality. In this way, Dean's example highlights how curricular standpoint has the potential to be effectively used with marginalized and dominant groups alike because it can be used to overcome epistemological resistance generally, regardless if the source of such resistance is based on marginalized or dominant social locations.

Mathematics Education I

An example of curricular standpoint in practice in mathematics education can be found in the work of Alexander and Munk (2010), who describe how at the "independent, girl-centered school for ... grades 1–12" (p. 52) where they work in Toronto, students combine mathematics, inquiry, and scientific method with an examination of social issues—which they summarize as social justice math:

> Social justice math ... begins with our curiosity about the world and especially about the world's unfairness. Thus a key part of the curriculum ... is promoting the habit of thoughtful questioning. In math classes, we use the inquiry process to reinforce the idea that knowledge is built from evidence that the students collect themselves.
>
> *(p. 52)*

In a process that clearly draws on Freire's (1974; Shor & Freire, 1987) work in literacy, Alexander and Munk (2010) ask students to go through a semi-structured process

where they identify issues of importance, develop some general questions surrounding those issues, refine their questions so that they can be explored/answered
using quantitative data, research and analyze the pertinent data, and develop and
share presentations of their questions and findings. The discussions that follow the
presentations are also a critical part of the process. As the authors explain:

> Students engage each other on the topics they researched, and on the math
> they used to analyze their data. They use their data management skills to
> justify their choices and defend their conclusions. We want students to feel
> that they have legitimate questions and comments to share about the math,
> about the thinking that their classmates were sharing.
>
> *(p. 54)*

The presentations and ensuing discussions comprise their school's annual social justice
data fair, which serves as the culmination of an extended mathematics unit.

Curricular standpoint readily apparent in Alexander and Munk's (2010) mathematics curriculum and social justice data fair. Immediately, Alexander and Munk
take up an explicitly feminist curricular standpoint, one that recognizes the broader
gender relations that exist within mathematics knowledge. They state:

> We teach girls, and girls have historically received messages that they are not
> good at math. These messages are often self-fulfilling. A social justice pedagogy,
> in addition to introducing social justice topics into the curriculum, must
> reduce barriers to learning for all students. It must engage students as agents of
> change in the world, and encourage them to view their skills—in math and
> elsewhere—as tools for enacting that change.
>
> *(p. 52)*

Thus, we see Alexander and Munk using the social location of the young women
in their school as the foundational underpinning for how they conceive of their
mathematics curriculum generally.

However, Alexander and Munk (2010) also recognize that the students' social
location as young women is simply the starting point for their mathematics
knowledge projects, and that it is important for the students to use other aspects of
their social locations as beginning points for their quantitative inquiries into social
issues—particularly if those inquiries are going to be meaningful for the students
themselves. Thus, extending from their positions as girls, these students move into
the realm of addressing social justice more generally through mathematics. This is a
critical curricular movement because not only do these young women challenge the
hegemonic gender relations within mathematics curricular knowledge, but they also
challenge the hegemonic construction of mathematics as an apolitical, neutral, and
value free discipline—a construction that does not validate mathematics as a tool for
social change. Consequently, Alexander and Munk's work also illustrates how

curricular standpoint in mathematics helps develop the potential for human liberation, as these young women are empowered by their increased mathematics literacy skills to develop critical consciousness around social issues they find important, thus increasing their potential to be involved in individual and social action on those very same issues.

Mathematics Education II

Another example of curricular standpoint in mathematics can be found in the work described by Yang (2009). Facilitating a youth Participatory Action Research (PAR) project where students critically consumed and critically produced mathematics texts, Yang details a process of how students developed generative themes in mathematics, searched for texts aligned with these themes, engaged with these texts through mathematical computation, writing assignments, and discussion, and finally developed project presentations that focused on data analysis, multimedia representation of data, and public presentation of data.

By nature of the student population and the pedagogy of Yang's (2009) work, this mathematics PAR project cannot help but illustrate curricular standpoint in practice. Demographically, the group of 30 students Yang worked with was over half Latino and nearly half African American, all of whom would be considered low achieving by typical academic criteria. By pedagogically relying on these students to develop generative themes for their own research projects, Yang effectively honored the standpoint of these students as individuals, but also as members of their respective cultural communities. This standpoint can be seen in the content of the themes themselves. As Yang explains:

> Some generative themes of greatest concern were their identities as raced-classed-gendered math learners, the absence or presence of culture and history in math, the oppressive nature of institutional mathematics, the applicability of math to social justice, problem solving methodologies, theories of numbers and numerology, and the epistemology of mathematics. Therefore, we searched for texts that corresponded to these themes.
>
> (p. 106)

The standpoint of these students is also apparent in the public presentations of their data analysis at the Social Justice in Mathematics Conference in New York. For instance, student presenter Michael Navarro remarked,

> Our cultures are misrepresented in the mainstream and in education. At our school, we learn where mathematics originated, and how relatively easy the methods we learn are compared to how our ancestors had to struggle and work through the math.
>
> (pp. 114–15)

Michael later adds that,

> By learning about your ancestors, you are going back to your roots and figuring out what your culture is … and the things that your culture used to do before we were colonized. We need to learn about how we used to be and then critically analyze how we can apply that to our daily modern lives.
>
> *(p. 115)*

Commenting on Michael's observation, Yang explains:

> By "the methods we learn," he was referring to the development of algebra and its familiar textbook steps in problem-solving algorithms, compared to the Kemetic [original Egyptian] methods of aha calculus that required precise error estimations or the calculations of the Maya whose unparalleled astronomical measurements were conducted without the benefit of fractions. His statements also reflected several layers of identity formation common in student writing: an identification with ancient African and Maya mathematicians, a view of self within mathematics education as a collective project, and an implicit identification of self as a math learner with a hard work ethic.
>
> *(p. 115)*

Yang also describes another student, Monique, and her summative conclusion of what social justice in mathematics means. He observes,

> For Monique, it was the pragmatics of self-determination. She described "three aspects of social justice in mathematics." She termed "economic self-determination" as requiring an education to provide tools for the financial well-being of the larger community, "representational self-determination" as providing the tools for people to shape their own identities, and educational self-determination as providing an opportunity structure for the collective advancement of oppressed people.
>
> *(p. 115)*

Yang's (2009) work with this youth PAR-based mathematics curriculum clearly demonstrates curricular standpoint. First, by nature of relying on a process of developing generative themes, this mathematics curriculum uses students' social locations as its starting point. Second, particularly in the case of Michael Navarro, we see how this curriculum challenged the status quo, hegemonic epistemologies surrounding mathematical knowledge, as Michael found significant academic and cultural benefit in learning about the multicultural origins of mathematical knowledge. Third, both Michael and Monique experienced/constructed curricular standpoint through the connection of mathematics to their social realities. In Michael's case, he recognized the incongruence between cultural foundations of mathematical knowledge usually taught in the curriculum versus the diverse, multicultural, and conceptually advanced mathematical knowledge as it existed historically. This incongruence is a manifestation of a racist, structurally Euro-centric presentation of mathematics—an example of the struggle over the social reality connected to mathematical epistemology itself. Indeed, we could say that Michael was able to develop a stronger, more objective account of mathematical knowledge itself. In Monique's case, her strong assertion that mathematics for social justice involves both economic self-determination and the expression of identity through representational self-determination speaks to where social reality connects to this mathematics curriculum. Clearly for her, economic self-determination is an issue that either she and/or her community has struggled with—as detailed by Yang in the social, economic, and educational context he paints in his research. The same can be said of Monique's call for representational self-determination, particularly when it is all too common for students to struggle with maintaining their cultural identities amidst the colonizing discourses often found in many public schools (Au, 2009b; Gillborn, 2005; Ladson-Billings & Tate IV, 1995)—all of which is a concrete manifestation of Monique's stronger, more objective engagement with school knowledge and community conditions as part of the curricular standpoint of this particular youth PAR project.

Fourth, for the students involved with the PAR described by Yang (2009), their mathematics curricular standpoint represents an achievement on multiple levels. From the perspective of mathematical skills, students achieved a high level of mathematical literacy, one that challenged the normative assumptions of low achievement often laid at the feet of working class Black and Latino youth. From the perspective of the politics of curricular knowledge, these PAR students also had to struggle with and overcome the hegemonic presentation of mathematical knowledge they experienced prior to participating in this program—resulting, for example, in Michael's commitment to a more culturally relevant mathematics instruction and Monique's commitment to educational self-determination.

Fifth and finally, the mathematics curriculum these students experienced/developed exhibited the potential for action towards liberation. One aspect can be seen in the presentation of research data phase of the PAR projects. By presenting their data, students are in effect taking one step towards action—sharing knowledge is one effective way of organizing people to take collective action and spur social change. The potential for liberation also lays in the content of their projects. Monique's articulation of social justice mathematics revolving around different types of self-determination is critical here: Internalizing the very concept of being able to take control of one's life and uplift one's community is powerfully liberating, and opens the door for Monique to be involved in developing "an opportunity structure for the collective advancement of oppressed people" (Yang, 2009, p. 115). Indeed, the potential for liberation is explicit in the PAR model: Participatory action research invites students to use their social locations as the basis for the action of inquiry and the action for change. PAR is, in many ways, the embodiment of praxis, of students using conceptual tools to interact dialectically with the knowledge structured in their educational environments.

Social Studies/History Education

"Rethinking the U.S. Constitutional Convention" (Peterson, 2001) provides an example of curricular standpoint in the social studies. This role play is built upon the questions: "Who benefited most (and the least) from the American Revolution? Who wrote and ratified the Constitution for the new nation? Who benefited most (and least) from the Constitution?" (Peterson, 2001, p. 63). Structurally, this role play is a mock U.S. Constitutional Convention with a twist: Groups who were not invited to the original U.S. Constitutional Convention are invited to this rethought one. Thus, the groups invited to the governmental negotiation table for this role play not only consist of "Male Southern Plantation Owners" and "Northern Merchants and Bankers" (which represent the bulk of the actual, historical attendees), but also include "White Workers/Indentured Servants," "Enslaved African Americans," "Free African Americans," "White Women," and "Native Americans—Iroquois Nation" (pp. 66–69).

In this lesson students are broken into the seven above-named groups. Once there, they are asked to read and understand their roles, as well as develop answers to two key questions regarding the new constitution: (1) "Should slavery and the slave trade be abolished, and should escaped slaves be returned to their owners?" and (2) "Who should be allowed to vote in our new nation, and especially what role should gender, race, and property ownership play in such a decision?" (Peterson, 2001, p. 65). After each group has developed their respective positions on these two questions, the lesson plan requires that one or two negotiators be selected from each group to travel to other groups in order to build alliances or determine who might be against them (and what their arguments might be). After the negotiating is completed, students return to their groups, and each group develops a speech to deliver to the Convention. As facilitator of the Convention, the teacher then poses the first question regarding slavery, taking statements from each group and allowing for a debate to take place. Once the debate has continued for a while, the teacher-facilitator then asks for groups to make formal proposals regarding the question of slavery. The same process is completed for the second question, and then the whole Convention votes. As is important with any role play, once completed, students are asked to reflect both on their individual "performance" and also on the issues raised: in this case issues of racism, sexism, and classism.

Even though Petersen works with many working class students of color and this role play could potentially validate their communities' perspectives on history and the world, this particular role play stands apart from his students' specific identities and thus could be taught to all kinds of students with powerful, yet understandably different effect. Thus we can still see curricular standpoint in Peterson's (2001) role play. First, it functionally takes up the standpoint of the oppressed in U.S. history and in the history curriculum—essentially asking students to take up historical standpoint relative to the social relations bound in the U.S. Constitution. Additionally, by including White women, free and enslaved Africans, poor Whites/indentured servants, and Native Americans in this rethought Constitutional Convention, Peterson explicitly recognizes the social locations of the "founding fathers" as being a very elite group of land owning, White males. Further, in making such a recognition, this role play challenges the validity of the socially located epistemologies of the "founding fathers" through the inclusion of the standpoint of marginalized, oppressed, and literally disenfranchised groups from that point in history. Consequently, by being grounded in the epistemological standpoint of these historically marginalized groups, Peterson's role play represents a form of achievement in that it actively challenges the hegemonic, status quo curriculum that generally disregards the social location of the "founding fathers" as being of importance (while simultaneously shunning the implications of their race, class, and gender status in favor of a constructed discourse of individual equality in the U.S. Constitution generally). In this sense, Peterson's role play validates the epistemologies of marginalized and oppressed groups from that time, and does so in a way that raises fundamental questions about equality in the United States both historically and contemporarily—thus revealing unequal social and material relations relative to politics and political structures in the United States. Further, we might also say that Peterson uses his curriculum to ultimately challenge the epistemology of the "founding fathers," many of whom were slave owners and/or benefitted from the taking of indigenous lands, and who somehow neglected to grant citizenship and/or voting rights to women, poor Whites, those of African descent (free or enslaved), and Native Americans. Finally, Peterson's role play helps create the potential for action towards liberation in that it develops students' critical consciousness about power relations within political systems, systems which carry manifest profound inequalities today.

Conclusion: The Concreteness of Curricular Standpoint

Of course, examples of curricular standpoint abound, and the point here has not been to highlight these particular examples as the only ones. These merely represent examples found in major school disciplines and across grade levels, and there are other examples that exist in these and other disciplines/subject areas. In this regard, it is important that I note that, while it is relatively easy to find a large number of examples of curricular standpoint in the social sciences and humanities, and, thankfully, there is a growing number of very good examples to be found in mathematics education, it was much more difficult to find concrete examples of curricular standpoint in practice in science education (in my search of the literature, while there have been several pieces of research done on the issue, they either suffered from a thin conception of social justice/critical consciousness, weak framing of the "science" in science education, or did not focus on classroom practice). However, there is a substantial amount of curricular standpoint in practice in most corners of

Taylor & Francis Group
an informa business

MASTER PACKING SLIP

Page 1

Send Returns To:
Taylor & Francis
C/O LSC Returns
5530 W 74th Street
Indianapolis, IN 46268

BILL TO:

L41001
May Jadallah
1210 E. Grove St.
APT. 302
Bloomington IL 61701

SHIP TO:

L41001
May Jadallah
1210 E. Grove St.
APT. 302
Bloomington IL 61701

PO Number	Account Number	Order Number	Shipment #	Date
04820152-0001	L41001	COE8406302	COE8406302	8/25/21

Item Number	Description	Order Qty	Ship Qty	List Price
9780415877121	CRITICAL CURRICULUM STUDIES EDUCATI	1	1	48.95

education. Between the various curriculum collections mentioned earlier in this chapter and the social justice teaching that is taking place increasingly in the United States and around the world (Apple, Au, & Gandin, 2009), any time educators take up a pedagogy of the oppressed (Freire, 1974) in a serious manner, they have to also think in terms of curricular standpoint.

Fundamentally, the point of this chapter has been to illustrate, in concrete terms, that not only is curricular standpoint practical and "doable" at the classroom level, it is also critically necessary if we are interested in revealing the (more objective) reality of unequal social relations and challenge the epistemological hegemony of dominant groups. In this sense, another point of my analysis here has been to illustrate the explanatory power of curricular standpoint on two levels. First, as I discussed in the previous chapter, I feel that progressive and social justice educators have, in general, undertheorized and explained what is "underneath" so much of their curriculum. Thus I've articulated curricular standpoint as a framework that offers some explanatory power for understanding what it is that these educators do in their curriculum (and I count myself among "these educators"). Second, the examples offered in this chapter illustrate the explanatory power of curricular standpoint as a methodological tool for analysis. In this regard I've offered these examples and the subsequent discussion as both form and function of curricular standpoint.

Further, I think it is important to look at these examples of curricular standpoint in practice in light of the conception of curriculum I developed in Chapter 3. To recap: the curriculum can be conceived of as the tool that structures the accessibility of knowledge in environmental form, where framing and classification communicate the accessibility and structure of knowledge, respectively. Curricular standpoint essentially recognizes that power relations structure the accessibility of educational environments, as well as the pedagogic discourse that is produced to communicate those relations. As the examples here illustrate, curricular standpoint, by using the social location of the marginalized or oppressed as its starting point for engaging with knowledge, effectively works to make particular knowledge (and epistemologies) accessible to students vis-à-vis educational environments that potentially validate the social, economic, cultural, and political experiences of those same marginalized or oppressed communities. This happens through the revealing of material reality and the systematic inequalities produced by social structures. In doing so, curricular standpoint invites learners from all social locations to understand the relationships of themselves and others to the totality of human social, economic, cultural, and political relations as well. In this sense, curricular standpoint invites learners to develop the meta-understandings that define critical consciousness (as discussed in Chapter 3), and point to the connections between curriculum and critical consciousness more generally. These connections are crucial to *Critical Curriculum Studies*, and are dealt with in the final chapter.

6

CONCLUSION: CRITICAL CONSCIOUSNESS, RELATIVE AUTONOMY, AND THE CURRICULUM

In *Critical Curriculum Studies* I have made a series of arguments about the relationships between epistemology, curriculum, and the politics of knowledge, in the process advancing a conception of what I've called curricular standpoint. I began with a discussion of tensions within curriculum studies (Chapter 1) and followed with an explanation of the dialectics of consciousness, essentially framing out a dynamic, interactional, and inseparable relationship between humans and our social and physical environments (Chapter 2). I then discussed what amounts to two implications of this conception of consciousness. First, I took up what it means for how we think about the curriculum, arguing for a definition/conception of curriculum as a form of complex environmental design (Chapter 3). Second, I interrogated how the social nature of consciousness and knowledge implicate the politics of the curriculum, resulting in my application of standpoint theory to curriculum studies (Chapter 4) and curricular practice (Chapter 5). In the process, I have brought critical theory and critical application to curriculum studies in a unique way and made some headway in advancing a theoretical justification and explanation of teaching for social justice by actively including the standpoint of the marginalized or oppressed in the curriculum. In a sense, and as I alluded to in the title of Chapter 5, I essentially argued for the necessity of teaching a curriculum of the oppressed, an argument that hinges on the idea that there is some relationship between what we learn (or what knowledge we access in our educational environments) and our consciousness, which in turn also relates to our praxis in the world.

Curriculum and Consciousness

The relationship between curriculum and consciousness has been central to my discussion and analysis here. In some ways there is nothing new about my focus

Curriculum to shape student consciousness about themselves & the world.

because fundamentally, the intent of all curriculum is to influence student learning and, by extension, shape student consciousness about not only subject matter, but also their worldview and their view of themselves. This may sound like a dastardly and conspiratorial idea, that critical and radical educators are somehow scheming and conniving to brainwash the impressionable young minds in their classrooms vis-à-vis our curriculum. But ultimately my point about curriculum intentionally shaping student consciousness is a fact of all education, and it has little to do with the specific political commitments (explicit or implicit) of any given teacher or text or policy. For example, a mathematics teacher, in working with students to learn mathematical thinking and relating to the world, is literally using the curriculum as a tool to shape student consciousness about mathematics and how it is used. Literally speaking, using mathematics curriculum to aid a student's learning to add or understand algebraic expressions (or any other mathematical concept/relationship) is effectively changing a student's consciousness about mathematics, as well as potentially changing their very thinking process. As educators, when we push students to learn something, to think about a subject more deeply and complexly, to consider some new or contradictory information, then in the broadest terms we are functionally involved in affecting student consciousness. In social studies education, as another example, there are many who argue powerfully that the social studies curriculum should instill strong notions of civic participation, citizenship, and democracy (Hess, 2009; Parker, 2005), and many social studies teachers are committed to this in their instruction. Now, academics may disagree about the nuances of this argument for the social studies, and some radically conservative groups may oppose teaching in this manner. However, a large swath of the political mainstream would have no qualms about a social studies curriculum that structures the accessibility of knowledge in a way that develops student consciousness towards civic participation—with no second thoughts, hesitation, or reservations at all. Teaching and learning are fundamentally about influencing student epistemology and consciousness, and, generally speaking, as long as what students are being taught and how it is being taught fall within the boundaries of the hegemonic commonsense of those in power locally or regionally, then the types of consciousness the curriculum fosters and develops in students tends to go unchallenged (Apple, 1995, 2000).

However, when the structure of the curriculum and the process of accessing knowledge embedded in environmental form challenge existing power relations and/or seem to land beyond the bounds of hegemonic commonsense, the idea of influencing student consciousness is framed as brainwashing or indoctrination or simply meets resistance. Examples of this process abound, including the examples of high-stakes testing and tracking I discussed in Chapter 4. The Rightward, conservative shift in mainstream U.S. politics and educational policy over the last 30-plus years (Apple, 2006) has produced some exemplars, however. For instance, the rise of conservative, evangelical forms of Christianity in the United States has resulted in ongoing controversy about whether or not (or how) science textbooks and science teachers should portray natural selection (evolution) versus the religiously based concept of intelligent design (Au, 2006–7; Hess, 2006; Scott & Branch, 2006). The arguments about this issue have illustrated that within some communities, the scientific concept of natural selection falls outside of the bounds of commonsense and where intelligent design is included within the bounds of commonsense. In such communities, then, science teachers and schools have found themselves under attack for designing curricular environments that foster a science-based consciousness that includes evolution as a key concept of biology. As such, in many cases the conservative, evangelical Christian parents and religious activists have changed textbook content and influenced the science curriculum to either challenge the validity of natural selection or include the religion-based concept of intelligent design as an equally competing explanation for biological diversity and evolution. What is fundamentally at risk for these conservative, evangelical Christian communities is the consciousness of their children, because in this case the concept of natural selection contradicts biblical interpretations of how the Earth was created.

The same can be said of the ideological struggle over the Texas Board of Education (TBE) state standards for social studies that took place in 2010. The TBE revisits the standards for teaching different subjects each year on a rotating basis, such that the social studies standards, for instance, are revised every 10 years. In 2010, the TBE had a very powerful conservative, evangelical Christian voting bloc of 7 of the total 15 board members, with other TBE republicans often voting to support this bloc's initiatives (Shorto, 2010).

Among others, in their revision of the state social studies standards, the conservatively controlled TBE removed the Seneca Falls Convention as well as women's suffrage activist, Carrie Chapman Catt from the standards. They also removed Harriet Tubman from the list of examples of good citizenship, and increased the inclusion of Christianity throughout. Further, the revised standards downplayed slavery and discussed it mainly in terms of how it shaped regions and precipitated the Civil War. Other changes included swapping Martin Luther King Jr. Day with Veterans' Day as holidays students should know about; removing Thomas Jefferson from a list of people whose writings inspired revolutions; minimizing the incarceration and internment of Japanese Americans during World War II; removing food, clothing, and shelter from the list of basic human needs; and changing the word "capitalism" to the phrase "free enterprise" throughout, while only emphasizing capitalism's perceived benefits (Bigelow, 2010; Foner, 2010; McKinley Jr., 2010).

As Foner (2010) explains in his sharp summary of the TBE social studies standards:

> More interesting is what the new standards tell us about conservatives' overall vision of American history and society and how they hope to instill that vision in the young. … Judging from the updated social studies curriculum, conservatives want students to come away from a Texas education with a favorable impression of: women who adhere to traditional gender roles, the Confederacy, some parts of the Constitution, capitalism, the military and religion. They do not think students should learn about women who

demanded greater equality; other parts of the Constitution; slavery, Reconstruction and the unequal treatment of nonwhites generally; environmentalists;
labor unions; federal economic regulation; or foreigners.

(p. 5)

This conservative vision of U.S. history mattered to the TBE and the constituencies
who voted them into office because the conservative members of the board were
concerned about student consciousness and epistemology as they learn about and
subsequently act within the world. As TBE member and self proclaimed Christian
activist Cynthia Dunbar explained, "The philosophy of the classroom in one generation will be the philosophy of the government in the next" (as quoted in,
Shorto, 2010, n.p.).

The conservative politics of the TBE matter nationally because, with a \$22-billion
education fund in 2010 and the purchase or distribution of 48 million textbooks
annually, the State of Texas represents one of the largest textbook markets in
the country. Thus, even though digital printing has limited its effect to some
degree, the State of Texas is still influential in its ability to shape textbook content
nationally as publishers curry favor to grab a share of such a large market (Shorto,
2010). Thus, as publishers seek to maximize profits through a large purchase by the
State of Texas, in some critical ways Texas' textbooks in part become the nation's
textbooks.

However, while the TBE members are quite powerful publicly, it is also
important to recognize that textbook negotiations with conservative TBE members
happen out of the public eye. Shorto (2010) relays the story of archconservative
TBE member Don McLeroy and how textbook publishers came to him directly for
input on their language arts textbooks:

> Last fall, McLeroy was frank in talking about how he applies direct pressure
> to textbook companies. In the language-arts re-evaluation, the members
> of the Christian bloc wanted books to include classic myths and fables rather
> than newly written stories whose messages they didn't agree with. They didn't
> get what they wanted from the writing teams, so they did an end run around
> them once the public battles were over. "I met with all the publishers,"
> McLeroy said. "We went out for Mexican food. I told them this is what we
> want. We want stories with morals, not P.C. stories." He then showed me an
> e-mail message from an executive at Pearson, … indicating the results of his
> effort: "Hi Don. Thanks for the impact that you have had on the development
> of Pearson's Scott Foresman Reading Street series. Attached is a list of some
> of the Fairy Tales and Fables that we included in the series."

(n.p.)

What we see through the Texas example is the way the politics of state decision-
making bodies manifest within the state standards, which in turn manifest in

the content of textbooks, which in turn enter into classroom curriculum vis-à-vis the textbooks. Indeed, Texas illustrates how state standards are themselves a part of the curriculum. Further, the Texas example also illustrates how such curriculum is promoted with the express intent of structuring educational environments to make certain knowledge more accessible than other knowledge, with the intent of influencing student consciousness. The fundamental issue at play is what types of consciousness based on which politics of rule (Bernstein, 1990).

It is important to note that the TBE was critiqued in parts of Texas and around the country, so the politics of the TBE did have its limits within regional commonsense. However, it is equally important to recognize that the TBE is a democratically elected board, and that conservative members, like Don McElroy, had served multiple terms—so their politics were likely known amongst voters from previous revisions of the state standards. Additionally, despite national critiques, while Texas provides a shining star of an example of conservative curriculum and hegemonic consciousness, it is important to note that it doesn't shine as a lone star. As Bigelow (2010) points out, the social studies standards of his home state of Oregon share many of the same overall pro-capitalist, individualist, and nationalist politics as Texas. In California's standards, Sleeter (2004) finds an explicit support for manifest destiny and an assumption that students should identify with a Western, Judeo-Christian "we" against a non-Western, non-Judeo-Christian "them." Similarly, as Rodriguez (2010) explains, the Arizona Department of Education banned the teaching of ethnic studies and Arizona State Superintendent of Schools Tom Horne has openly maintained that the only knowledge that should be taught in schools should be that which originated in Western or Greco-Roman civilization. Indeed, as of January 1, 2011, Horne declared the Latino studies courses in Tuscon schools and the rest of the state to be illegal (Lacey, 2011). Thus, even if the social standards edited and promoted by the TBE are particularly outrageous and have stirred public controversy (in some places), the politics of knowledge (and, by extension, the politics of consciousness) have been contested and swayed by conservative forces at the highest levels of education policy and curriculum development.

The Relative Autonomy of Consciousness and Curricular Structure

Despite the hegemonic, conservative politics generally found in the "official knowledge" (Apple, 2000) of state standards and textbooks (taking for granted that much curriculum can also contain progressive elements), it is critical to recognize that the politics of such curricular tools are not simply poured into the heads of students such that they robotically parrot the knowledge they access within the curricular environments with which they interact. Rather, as I stressed in Chapter 2, and wish to stress again here, the dialectical conception of consciousness does not posit a mechanical or deterministic relationship between the environment and consciousness. The environment does not have a simple, linear, cause-and-effect relationship with consciousness. There is unevenness. There is push and pull. There

كل ما ولدت
انحطاط الوعي
المعنى لدى
الطلبة
تفنى أمن

لفائدة بصورة ميكانيكية وهذا

(سبب-قدر) الموضوع الجدلي لوعي ليس مستويا أو بسظو و ميكانيكا
تفاعل
هناك علاقة شائبة سبب، أنا دعاها، قبول ورفض، هناك دفع وجذب

is tension. There is dynamism and fluidity. There is interaction. Humans and human consciousness are constantly developing in relation to each other and changing each other as well. As such, it is important to understand that consciousness essentially has a relatively autonomous relationship with curricular structures.

Addressing the relative autonomy of consciousness requires consideration of a fundamental relationship. As I discussed in Chapter 2, if consciousness "is actively produced within our experience of our social, material and cultural existence," as Allman (1999, p. 37) suggests, is consciousness thus totally determined by external material and social factors, or do humans have the capability to determine how they think about and "know" the world around them? This question correlates with a parallel question about the relationship between schools and consciousness more broadly, one that has been asked by many critical educational scholars with varying effect (see, e.g., Apple, 2004; Bernstein, 1996; Bourdieu & Passeron, 1977; Bowles & Gintis, 1976; Giroux, 1980). Namely: Do schools simply reproduce the unequal social and economic relations associated with capitalism, or can they exist as sites of critical social and cultural resistance to status quo inequalities?

The parallel between these two questions can be found in their mutual inter-rogation of the relationship between ideas and material reality. In the case of human consciousness, we are dealing with how human thinking relates to and extends from interaction with the material world. In the case of education, we are dealing with how schools, as sites of knowledge construction/reconstruction and as sites of cul-tural production/reproduction, relate to and extend from the material social and economic relations that exist externally to schools themselves (Apple, 1995; Au, 2009f). When we look at both consciousness and schools, we certainly see external relations impinging upon the structures of both. In terms of con-sciousness, for instance, work in the sociology of school knowledge outlines how pedagogic discourse—literally, the communicative discourse in classroom settings—functions to regulate how students see and understand the world through the reg-ulation of the knowledge they interact with/are taught in that discourse (Au, 2008c; Bernstein, 1996). In this regard, the external social, cultural, and material environ-ment holds significant (but not total) power over how student consciousness is formed.

In terms of schools, nearly any statistic related to educational outcomes will bear out the ways external social and economic relations encroach: Students of color, as well as low income students of all colors, have lower test scores, lower graduation rates, higher drop out rates, and higher disciplinary rates than their White, higher income counterparts (see, e.g., Ladson-Billings, 2006; Laird, Lew, DeBell, & Chapman, 2006; Nichols & Berliner, 2007; Sirin, 2005). Indeed, as Berliner's (2009) analysis suggests, significant out-of-school factors such as inadequate healthcare, food insecurity, and environmental pollutants, among others, oftentimes limit what schools can accomplish on their own in regards to student success or failure. Thus it would seem that schools are structured to simply reproduce the inequalities we see in society more broadly.

Other educational research, however, also challenges the idea that schools simply reproduce inequality. For instance, as Apple (1995, 2004) and Carnoy and Levin (1985) explain, despite reproducing socio-economic inequalities in a general sense, schools also play the somewhat contradictory role of legitimating ideologies of individual equality and meritocracy. Additionally, there is ample evidence that students (see, e.g., Dance, 2002; Shor, 1992; Willis, 1977) and teachers (see, e.g., Allman, McLaren, & Rikowski, 2000; Carlson, 1988) resist the structuring forces of schooling in both cultural and material ways. Indeed, significant portions of this resistance can be directly attributed to the ideology of equality that the schools themselves help maintain.

These seemingly contradictory relations embodied by schools—largely reproducing external socio-economic inequalities while simultaneously producing resistance to those very same inequalities—speaks to the "relative autonomy" of education from capitalist socio-economic relations (Althusser, 1971; Apple, 1995; Au, 2006). Thus, even though "in the last analysis" (Gramsci, 1971, p. 162) or "in the last instance" (Althusser, 1971, p. 135), the dominant economic relation "finally asserts itself as necessary" (Engels, 1968, p. 692) and structure schooling in a broad sense, the relatively autonomous positioning of schools also means that they are not totally structured by outside forces: that sites of alternative relations and resistance functionally exist within schools as well (Au, 2006, 2009f; Bernstein, 1996). Indeed, all of the examples of curricular standpoint discussed in Chapter 5 illustrate this relatively autonomous relationship because, despite the fact that they have been taught in schools structured by external relations, the curricular standpoint of those examples sought to fundamentally challenge those very same relations.

A similar argument can and should be made regarding consciousness and the curriculum. Consciousness cannot be understood as a linear, mechanical reflection of curricular structure and educational experience, nor as completely determined by curricular structure and educational experience. What the structure of the curriculum can do is promote certain forms of consciousness as viable, appropriate, beneficial, and "right" (or, conversely, as unviable, inappropriate, detrimental, and "wrong")— thus working in the realms of hegemonic, commonsense understanding (Gramsci, 1971) and meta-reflections on the world (Vygotsky, 1987). Thus, both the politics of curriculum and the politics of consciousness are fundamentally at issue, and put in the simplest of terms, consciousness is relatively autonomous from the way knowledge is structured and accessed in the curriculum. Curricular structures can and do influence student consciousness, but as humans we have the capacity to think critically and potentially to accept or reject the forms of consciousness that curriculum seeks to foster.

The relatively autonomous relationship between consciousness and the curriculum also speaks recursively back to two central pieces of *Critical Curriculum Studies*. First, it functionally speaks to the positivist/post-modern (pragmatic/subjectivist) tensions that have existed historically within curriculum studies and that I discussed in Chapter 1. The forms of knowledge the curriculum encompasses and the selective access and distribution of that knowledge (and, subsequently, the selective access, distribution, and validation of epistemologies) the curriculum carries with it, essentially point to the social, political, and material realities of classroom relations and school life. In a parallel and conjoined manner, the relative autonomy of consciousness fundamentally points to the subjectivity of individual identity and sense-making within the learning process. Put differently, we might say that the curriculum (and curricular form) structures but doesn't completely determine consciousness. Likewise we might also say that consciousness acts reflexively and subjectively back on curriculum but is never totally freed from its structures. In this way, the relative autonomy of consciousness and the curriculum intercedes in the debates within the field of curriculum studies because it allows for a certain amount of epistemological subjectivity, but also allows for the recognition of a certain amount of material structuration of epistemology as well. Indeed, this relationship lies at the root of the dialectical conception of consciousness I offered in Chapter 2.

Similarly, the second way that the relative autonomy of consciousness and the curriculum speaks back to the central arguments undertaken in this book is through the curricular standpoint. By carrying the dialectical conception of consciousness forward into the politics of knowledge in the curriculum, curricular standpoint embraces the subjectivity of students' social locations (as well as how those locations impact epistemology), but does so in a way that also embraces the material realities that essentially produced those social locations to begin with. Curricular standpoint thus asks students to critically reflect on their own subjective individual and collective experiences, but to do such reflection relative to the materiality of social, economic, cultural, and other structural forces that exist in their (and our) lives. In this way curricular standpoint effectively addresses both the politics of recognition and the politics of redistribution (Fraser, 1995) and consequently embodies the relative autonomy of consciousness and the curriculum.

The Critical Re-Turn of Curriculum Studies

In this book I've entered into the scholarly debate surrounding the field of curriculum studies, its direction, and its future. I've argued that if curriculum studies is to gain and maintain relevance with regards to education and what happens in schools, then the field would be well-served by interrogating issues that are critically relevant to contemporary educational and social conditions, with particular attention paid to how power and inequality manifests in their myriad forms. The framework for curricular standpoint I've conceptualized and put into brief practice here offers one way (and only one among many possibilities) for the field of curriculum studies to find such critical relevance. As such, I hope to have provided a powerful conceptual tool for justifying the privileging of marginalized or oppressed groups in curriculum studies as part of an appeal to understanding material and social reality as it exists in ways that are more truthful and more objective than those with which hegemonic perspectives provide us. Curricular standpoint thus calls for the revitalization of the field of curriculum studies as a critical, intervening force in the struggle against the problems in our schools that have manifested themselves during the period of conservative modernization (Apple, 2006; Valenzuela, 2005a). In some important ways, curricular standpoint thus seeks a return to understanding curriculum as what has been referred to by scholars as both a "political text" and an "institutional text," even while some have declared these paradigms in curriculum theory to be dead or collapsed (see Pinar, 1998; Pinar, Reynolds, Slattery, & Taubman, 1995). If the field of curriculum studies would like to find its relevance and have an impact, it would do well for scholars in the field to weigh in on politically important issues in schools and communities. However, to do so requires that we return to examining the politics of the curriculum, develop a better understanding of the role that curriculum plays in the reproduction of inequitable social relations, support and constructively interrogate curriculum that successfully addresses the incorporation of material and social relations into school knowledge (e.g. social justice education and/or curricular standpoint), and develop elaborated theories that recognize the subjectivities of individual and collective experiences/identities, but also remain committed to classroom practice.

There is, of course, curriculum and consciousness and schools and politics and policy, but it is critical to remember that at the heart of this discussion are the students and how education relates to the human condition. I started *Critical Curriculum Studies* with my experience at Middle College High School and would like to end the book there as well. The more I reflect back on my students and the curriculum we taught there, the more I feel the weight of alienation that my students were feeling and that we, as their teachers, were desperately trying to overcome. Fundamentally our students were alienated from just about everything in their lives. They were often alienated from their families, with distressed relations defining their home lives more often than not. They certainly found themselves alienated from their educational experiences, where they couldn't find meaningful connection to teachers, school structures, and the curriculum. As I wrote in Chapter 4 regarding cultural relevance and curricular standpoint, you could say they were experiencing epistemological alienation in that their knowing was separated from their being. Most distressingly, they were alienated from their very selves, with many feeling as if they had no power over their own lives and their futures: Caught up in surviving the everyday experience, our students entered Middle College rarely understanding the big picture, the patterns, the social processes, the history, the institutional relationships operating through and manifesting in their lives.

As I discussed in Chapter 1, a highlight of our Middle College curriculum came in 1999 when the massive protests against the World Trade Organization (WTO) took place in Seattle, Washington. It was a powerful time to be in the city, with activists, demonstrators, and a whole lot of regular folks (e.g., families with babies in strollers) coming together to voice a collective opposition to the anti-democratic and anti-environmental economic policies of the WTO. To build for this event, and to help students make sense of the flurry of media surrounding both the meetings and the protests, we studied the WTO and how systems of free trade impacted not only the people and environments around the world, but also our students' lives and communities locally. We wanted our students to understand that the WTO wasn't just some far-flung organization in the abstract and that the resistance to WTO policies wasn't similarly distant—that there were bigger processes at play, that our students were in fact concretely connected to other folks halfway around the world, and that they could overcome some of their alienation and be a part of something bigger.

When the first official day of mass protests came, we shut down school. Many parents, out of fear of the general tumult of the day, simply told their children to stay home anyways. For some of us teachers, participating in the demonstrations was of critical importance, and we would have called in substitutes and taken sick days if we had to as well. Thus, even though we could in no way legally have a field trip to the WTO demonstrations, several of our students chose to meet us in downtown Seattle (and several others just went and we happened to see them around). Let me just say that, if you've never been to a demonstration with tens of thousands, (or better yet hundreds of thousands), I highly recommend it. It is a powerful experience that invites shifts in consciousness, which we saw in most of the students who participated in the protests. As one of our students, DJ Neebor, wrote in a reflective poem he entitled "Bombshells":

> Bombshells of canisters
> right for human slaves
> all brought together
> awaken people today
> inside this peaceful parade
> the righteous have been sprayed
> by an ignorant army
> in hopes of some delays
> but we stopped them
> we did
> delegates and corporate leaders
> the power of all
> a right to stand for freedom each
> and everyone took part
> in a march for human life
> took time from their work
> school and daily life
> for the innocent many
> who have not been given life
> we all laid arms down
> and offer ourselves to sacrifice

Neebor's poem is important in that it illustrates the way he made sense of the day's events. Of particular note is the way he connects himself with those facing injustice around the world and in the protests that day, as well as the power he experienced as the protests literally shut down the WTO meetings.

It is this type of connection we strove for with the Middle College curriculum, an antidote to our students' alienation. We wanted them to not be objects of history, but instead become subjects of history (Freire, 1974), even subjects of their own lives. So we connected our curriculum both to the specificities of their social locations as well as to the relations and processes that shaped their material existence. We studied how capitalism systematically produced (and relied upon) poverty. We tracked institutionalized racism in the justice system, housing, and employment. We looked at how systems of education have generally functioned to reproduce inequality. However, we also buttressed our study of systematic oppression with powerful stories of resistance. Our students learned about the Quilombos, where enslaved Africans escaped, formed communities in Brazil, and heroically fought back against the advancements of European colonizers. They also learned about the Black Panthers, the Brown Berets, and other groups who consciously and deliberately organized against racism and poverty in the United States historically. We taught them about unsung heroes like Yuri Kochiyama as well, a Japanese American woman who worked closely with Malcom X in Harlem and went onto live a life of resistance and activism. The examples are nearly endless, but the overall hope was that, if our students could figure out what was structuring their lives in such terribly alienating ways and see models of how people have overcome similar alienation, they could then also identify what power they had to negotiate those structures and make changes, both big and small, in their lives. In this regard, not only did our curriculum embody both curricular standpoint and the relative autonomy of curriculum and consciousness, we absolutely relied on our students' capacity to develop critical consciousness and potential to make life-altering decisions and actions. It may not have always worked. For some students, either the material conditions of their lives were simply too strong or their individual consciousness wasn't ready for the responsibility required to access their power. Internalized oppression and self-doubt were always difficult demons to exorcise, but when we did, when classroom conditions met consciousness, our curriculum worked wonders.

REFERENCES

Alexander, B., & Munk, M. (2010). A social justice data fair: Questioning the world through math. *Rethinking Schools, 25*(1), 51–54.

Allman, P. (1999). *Revolutionary social transformation: Democratic hopes, political possibilities and critical education* (1st ed.). Westport, CT: Bergin & Garvey.

Allman, P. (2007). *On Marx: An introduction to the revolutionary intellect of Karl Marx.* Rotterdam, The Netherlands: Sense Publishers.

Allman, P., McLaren, P., & Rikowski, G. (2000). After the box people: The labour-capital relation as class constitution—and its consequences for Marxist educational theory and human resistance. Retrieved May 1, 2004, from *http://www.ieps.org.uk.cwc.net/afterthebox.pdf*

Althusser, L. (1971). *Lenin and philosophy and other essays* (B. Brewster, Trans.). New York: Monthly Review Books.

Andre-Bechely, L. (2005). Public school choice at the intersection of voluntary integration and not-so-good neighborhood schools: Lessons from parents' experiences. *Educational Administration Quarterly, 41*(2), 267–305.

Anyon, J. (1980). Social class and the hidden curriculum of work. *Journal of Education, 162* (1), 67–92.

Apple, M. W. (1973). Curriculum design and cultural order. In N. Smimahara (Ed.), *Educational reconstruction: Promise and challenge* (pp. 157–83). Columbus, OH: Charles E. Merrill Publishing Company.

Apple, M. W. (1975). Scientific interests and the nature of educational institutions. In W. F. Pinar (Ed.), *Curriculum theorizing: The reconceptualists* (pp. 120–30). Berkeley, CA: McCutchan Publishing.

Apple, M. W. (1978). Ideology and form in curriculum evaluation. In G. Willis (Ed.), *Qualitative evaluation* (pp. 495–521). Berkeley, CA: McCutchan Publishing Corporation.

Apple, 'M. W. (1986). *Teachers and texts: A political economy of class and gender relations in education.* New York: Routledge & Kegan Paul.

Apple, M. W. (1988). Social crisis and curriculum accords. *Educational Theory, 38*(2), 191–201.

Apple, M. W. (1995). *Education and power* (2nd ed.). New York: Routledge.

Apple, M. W. (2000). *Official knowledge: Democratic education in a conservative age* (2nd ed.). New York: Routledge.

Apple, M. W. (2004). *Ideology and curriculum* (3rd ed.). New York: RoutledgeFalmer.

Apple, M. W. (2006). *Educating the "right" way: Markets, standards, god, and inequality* (2nd ed.). New York: Routledge.

Apple, M. W. (2010a). Fly and the fly bottle: On Dwayne Huebner, the uses of language, and the nature of the curriculum field. *Curriculum Inquiry, 40*(1), 95–103. doi: 10.1111/j.1467–1873X.2009.00469.x

Apple, M. W. (2010b, December 7). [Personal communication.]

Apple, M. W., Au, W., & Gandin, L. A. (Eds.). (2009). *The Routledge international handbook of critical education.* New York: Routledge.

Apple, M. W., & Beyer, L. E. (1988). Social evaluation of curriculum. In L. E. Beyer & M. W. Apple (Eds.), *The curriculum: Problems, politics, and possibilities* (pp. 334–49). Albany: State University of New York Press.

Apple, M. W., & Christian-Smith, L. K. (1991). The politics of the textbook. In M. W. Apple & L. K. Christian-Smith (Eds.), *The politics of the textbook* (pp. 1–21). New York: Routledge.

Apple, M. W., & Whitty, G. (2002). Structuring the postmodern in education policy. In D. Hill, P. McLaren, & G. Rikowski (Eds.), *Marxism against postmodernism in educational theory* (pp. 67–88). Lanham, MD: Lexington Books.

Au, W. (2000). Teaching about the WTO. *Rethinking Schools, 14*(3), 4–5.

Au, W. (2005). Power, identity, and the third rail. In P. C. Miller (Ed.), *Narratives from the classroom: An introduction to teaching* (pp. 65–85). Thousand Oaks, CA: Sage Publications.

Au, W. (2006). Against economic determinism: Revisiting the roots of neo-Marxism in critical educational theory. *Journal for Critical Education Policy Studies, 4*(2). Retrieved December 12, 2006, from *http://www.jceps.com/?pageID=article=66.*

Au, W. (2006–7). Intelligent instruction needed. *Rethinking Schools, 21*(2), 56–57.

Au, W. (2007a). Epistemology of the oppressed: The dialectics of Paulo Freire's theory of knowledge. *Journal for Critical Education Policy Studies, 5*(2). Retrieved November 2, 2007, from *http://www.jceps.com/index.php?pageID=article=100.*

Au, W. (2007b). High-stakes testing and curricular control: A qualitative metasynthesis. *Educational Researcher, 36*(5), 258–67.

Au, W. (2007c). Vygotsky and Lenin on learning: The parallel structures of individual and social development. *Science & Society, 71*(3), 273–98.

Au, W. (2008a). Between education and the economy: High-stakes testing and the contradictory location of the new middle class. *Journal of Education Policy, 23*(5), 501–13.

Au, W. (2008b). Defending dialectics: Rethinking the neo-Marxist turn in critical education theory. In S. Macrine, P. McLaren, & D. Hill (Eds.), *Organizing pedagogy: Educating for social justice and socialism.* New York: Routledge.

Au, W. (2008c). Devising inequality: A Bernsteinian analysis of high-stakes testing and social reproduction in education. *British Journal of Sociology of Education, 29*(6), 639–51.

Au, W. (2009a). The "building tasks" of critical history: Structuring social studies for social justice. *Social Studies Research and Practice, 4*(2). Retrieved July 30, 2009, from *http://www.socstrp.org/issues/showissue.cfm?volID=5=11.*

Au, W. (2009b). Decolonizing the classroom: Lessons in multicultural education. *Rethinking Schools, 23*(2), 27–30.

Au, W. (2009c). Fighting with the text: Critical issues in the development of Freirian pedagogy. In M. W. Apple, W. Au, & L. A. Gandin (Eds.), *The Routledge handbook of critical education* (pp. 83–95). New York: Routledge.

Au, W. (2009d). High-stakes testing and discursive control: The triple bind for non-standard student identities. *Multicultural Perspectives, 11*(2), 65–71.

Au, W. (2009e). Social studies, social justice: W(h)ither the social studies in high-stakes testing? *Teacher Education Quarterly, 35*(1), 43–58.

Au, W. (2009f). *Unequal by design: High-stakes testing and the standardization of inequality.* New York: Routledge.

Au, W. (2010a). The idiocy of policy: The anti-democratic curriculum of high-stakes testing. *Critical Education, 1*(1), 1–16. Retrieved January 18, 2010, from http://m1.cust.educ.ubc.ca/journal/index.php/criticaled/issue/view/11

Au, W. (2010b). In defense of dialectics: Rethinking the neo-Marxist turn in critical educational theory. In S. Macrine, P. McLaren, & D. Hill (Eds.), *Revolutionizing pedagogy: Education for social justice within and beyond neo-liberalism* (pp. 145–66). New York: Palgrave.

Au, W. (2011). Teaching under the new Taylorism: High-stakes testing and scientific management in the 21st century curriculum. *Journal of Curriculum Studies, 43* (1), 25–45.

Au, W., & Apple, M. W. (2009a). The curriculum and the politics of inclusion and exclusion. In E. Tressou, S. Mitakidou, B. Swadener, C. Grant, & W. Secada (Eds.), *Beyond pedagogies of exclusion in diverse childhood contexts: Transnational challenges* (pp. 101–16). New York: PalgraveMacmillan.

Au, W., & Apple, M. W. (2009b). Rethinking reproduction: Neo-Marxism in critical educational theory. In M. W. Apple, W. Au, & L. A. Gandin (Eds.), *The Routledge handbook of critical education* (pp. 83–95). New York: Routledge.

Au, W., Bigelow, B., & Karp, S. (Eds.). (2007). *Rethinking our classrooms: Teaching for equity and justice* (Revised and Expanded, 2nd ed. Vol. 1). Milwaukee, WI: Rethinking Schools.

Bakhurst, D. (1991). *Consciousness and revolution in soviet philosophy: From the Bolsheviks to Evald Ilyenkov.* New York: Cambridge University Press.

Bakhurst, D. (1997). Activity, consciousness, and communication. In M. Cole, Y. Engestrom, & O. Vasquez (Eds.), *Mind, culture, and activity: Seminal papers from the laboratory of comparative human cognition* (pp. 147–63). Cambridge, UK: Cambridge University Press.

Ball, S. J. (2003a). *Class strategies and the education market: The middle classes and social advantage.* New York: RoutledgeFalmer.

Ball, S. J. (2003b). The teacher's soul and the terrors of performativity. *Journal of Education Policy, 18*(3), 215–28.

Ball, S. J. (2006). *Education policy and social class: The selected works of Stephen J. Ball.* London & New York: Routledge.

Banks, J. A. (2008). Diversity, group identity, and citizenship education in a global age. *Educational Researcher, 37*(3), 129–39.

Banks, J. A. (2009). Human rights, diversity, and citizenship education. *The Educational Forum, 73*(2), 100–10.

Beauchamp, G. A. (1982). Curriculum theory: Meaning, development, and use. *Theory Into Practice, 21*(1), 23–27.

Benton, T., & Craib, I. (2001). *Philosophy of social science: The philosophical foundations of social thought.* New York: Palgrave.

Berliner, D. C. (2009). *Poverty and potential: Out-of-school factors and school success.* Boulder, CO & Tempe, AZ: Education and the Public Interest Center & Educational Policy Research Unit.

Bernstein, B. B. (1977). *Class codes and control volume 3: Towards a theory of educational transmissions* (2nd ed.). London: Routledge and Kegan Paul.

Bernstein, B. B. (1990). *The structuring of pedagogic discourse* (1st ed. Vol. IV). New York: Routledge.

Bernstein, B. B. (1996). *Pedagogy, symbolic control, and identity: Theory, research, critique.* London: Taylor & Francis.

Bernstein, B. B. (1999). Official knowledge and pedagogic identities. In F. Christie (Ed.), *Pedagogy and the shaping of consciousness: Linguistic and social processes* (pp. 246–61). New York: Cassell.

Bernstein, B. B., & Solomon, J. (1999). 'Pedagogy, identity, and the construction of a theory of symbolic control': Basil Bernstein questioned by Joseph Solomon. *British Journal of Sociology of Education, 20*(2), 265–79.

Beyer, L. E., & Liston, D. P. (1992). Discourse or moral action? A critique of post-modernism. *Educational Theory, 42*(4), 371–93.

Beyer, L. E., & Liston, D. P. (1996). *Curriculum in conflict: Social visions, educational agendas, and progressive school reform.* New York: Teachers College Press.

Bhaskar, R. (1989). *Reclaiming reality: A critical introduction to contemporary philosophy* (2nd ed.). New York: Verso.

Bigelow, B. (1994). Getting off the track: Stories from an untracked classroom. In B. Bigelow, L. Christensen, S. Karp, B. Miner, & B. Peterson (Eds.), *Rethinking our classrooms: Teaching for equity and justice* (Vol. 1, pp. 58–65). Milwaukee, WI: Rethinking Schools.

Bigelow, B. (2006). *The line between us: Teaching about the border and Mexican immigration.* Milwaukee, WI: Rethinking Schools Ltd.

Bigelow, B. (2010). Those awful Texas social studies standards: And what about yours? *Rethinking Schools, 24*(4), 46–48.

Bloom, C. M., & Erlandson, D. A. (2003). African American women principals in urban schools: Realities, (re)constructions, and resolutions. *Educational Administration Quarterly, 39*(3), 339–69. doi: 0.1177/0013161X03253413.

Bobbitt, J. F. (1972 [1918]). *The curriculum.* New York: Arno Press.

Bourdieu, P. (1984). *Distinction: A social critique of the judgment of taste* (R. Nice, Trans.). Cambridge, MA: Routledge & Kegan Paul Ltd.

Bourdieu, P., & Passeron, J. (1977). *Reproduction in education, society, and culture.* Beverly Hills, CA: Sage.

Bowles, S., & Gintis, H. (1976). *Schooling in capitalist America: Educational reform and the contradictions of economic life* (1st ed.). New York: Basic Books.

Brantlinger, E. (2003). *Dividing classes: How the middle class negotiates and rationalizes school advantage* (1st ed.). New York: RoutledgeFalmer.

Broussard, A. C., & Joseph, A. L. (1998). Tracking: A form of educational neglect? *Social Work in Education, 20*(2), 110.

Brown, A. L. (2010). Counter-memory and race: An examination of African American scholars' challenges to early twentieth century K-12 historical discourses. *The Journal of Negro Education, 79*(1), 54–65.

Brown, A. L., & Campione, J. C. (1996). Psychological theory and the design of innovative learning environments: On procedures, principles, and systems. In L. Schauble & R. Glaser (Eds.), *Innovations in learning: New environments for education* (pp. 289–325). Mahwah, NJ: L. Erlbaum Associates.

Buras, K. L. (2007). Benign neglect? Drowning yellow buses, racism, and disinvestment in the city that Bush forgot. In K. J. Saltman (Ed.), *Schooling and the politics of disaster* (pp. 103–22). New York: Routledge.

Buras, K. L. (2008). *Rightist multiculturalism: Core lessons on neoconservative school reform.* New York: Routledge.

Burch, P. (2009). *Hidden markets: The new education privatization.* New York: Routledge.

Canagarajah, S. A. (2002). *A geopolitics of academic writing.* Pittsburgh, PA: University of Pittsburgh Press.

Carlson, D. L. (1988). Beyond the reproductive theory of teaching. In M. Cole (Ed.), *Bowles and Gintis revisited: Correspondence and contradiction in educational theory* (pp. 158–73). New York: The Falmer Press.

Carnoy, M., & Levin, H. M. (1985). *Schooling and work in the democratic state.* Stanford, CA: Stanford University Press.

Chau, M., Thampi, K., & Wight, V. R. (2010). *Basic facts about low-income children, 2009.* New York: National Center for Children in Poverty (Mailman School of Public Health at Columbia University).

Christensen, L. (2009a). Putting out the linguistic welcome mat. In W. Au (Ed.), *Rethinking multicultural education: Teaching for racial and cultural justice* (pp. 89–96). Milwaukee, WI: Rethinking Schools Ltd.

Christensen, L. (2009b). *Teaching for joy and justice: Reimagining the language arts classroom.* Milwaukee, WI: Rethinking Schools, Ltd.

Chunn, E. W. (1987–88). Sorting black students for success and failure: The inequality of ability grouping and tracking. *The Urban League Review, 11*(1, 2), 93–106.

Clarke, J., & Newman, J. (1997). *The managerial state: Power, politics and ideology in the remaking of social welfare*. London: SAGE Publications.

Cole, M., & Engeström, Y. (1997). A cultural-historical approach to distributed cognition. In G. Salomon (Ed.), *Distributed cognitions: Psychological and educational considerations* (pp. 1–46). Cambridge, UK: Cambridge University Press.

Cole, M., & Scribner, S. (1978). Introduction *Mind in society: By L.S. Vygotsky* (pp. 1–14). Cambridge, MA: Harvard University Press.

Collins, P. H. (2000). *Black Feminist thought: Knowledge, consciousness, and the politics of empowerment*. New York: Routledge.

Connell, R. W. (1994). *Schools and social justice*. Philadelphia: Temple University Press.

Cooper, C. W. (2005). School choice and the standpoint of African American mothers: Considering the power of positionality. *The Journal of Negro Education, 74*(2), 174–89.

Cornbleth, C., & Waugh, D. (1995). *The great speckled bird* (1st ed.). New York: St. Martin's Press.

Cornell, P. (2002). The impact of changes in teaching and learning on furniture and the learning environment. *New Directions for Teaching and Learning* (92), 33–42.

Counts, G. S. (1927/1969). *The social composition of boards of education: A study in the social control of public education*. New York: Arno Press & The New York Times.

Counts, G. S. (1932). *Dare the schools build a new social order?* New York: John Day.

Dagbovie, P. G. (2004). Making Black history practical and popular: Carter G. Woodson, the proto Black Studies Movement, and the struggle for Black liberation. *The Western Journal of Black Studies, 28*(2), 372–83.

Dagbovie, P. G. (2007). *The early black history movement, Carter G. Woodson, and Lorenzo Johnston Greene*. Urbana: University of Illinois.

Dance, J. L. (2002). *Tough fronts: The impact of street culture on schooling* (1st ed.). New York: RoutledgeFalmer.

Darder, A., & Torres, R. D. (2004). *After race: Racism after multiculturalism*. New York: New York University Press.

Davis, R., & Freire, P. (1981). Education for awareness: A talk with Paulo Freire. In R. Mackie (Ed.), *Literacy and revolution: The pedagogy of Paulo Freire* (pp. 57–69). New York: The Continuum Publishing Company.

Dean, J. (2007). Teaching about global warming in truck country. In W. Au, B. Bigelow, & S. Karp (Eds.), *Rethinking our classrooms: Teaching for equity and social justice* (Revised and Expanded ed., Vol. 1, pp. 57–62). Milwaukee, WI: Rethinking Schools.

DeLissovoy, N. (2008). Conceptualizing oppression in educational theory: Toward a compound standpoint. *Cultural Studies < = > Critical Methodologies, 8*(1), 82–105. doi: 10.1177/1532708607310794.

Denzin, N., & Lincoln, Y. (Eds.). (2000). *Handbook of qualitative research*. Thousand Oaks, CA: Sage.

Dewey, J. (1901). The situation as regards the course of study *Journal of Proceedings and Addresses of the Fortieth Annual Meeting* (pp. 332–48). Washington, DC: National Educational Association.

Dewey, J. (1902). *The child and the curriculum*. Chicago: University of Chicago Press.

Dewey, J. (1916). *Democracy and education* (Free Press Paperback, 1966 ed.). New York: The Free Press.

Dimitriadis, G., & McCarthy, C. (2001). *Reading & teaching the postcolonial: From Baldwin to Basquiat and beyond*. New York: Teachers College Press.

Dingerson, L. (2008). Unlovely: How the market is failing the children of New Orleans. In L. Dingerson, B. Miner, B. Peterson, & S. Walters (Eds.), *Keeping the promise? The debate over charter schools* (pp. 17–34). Milwaukee, WI: Rethinking Schools.

Dobrin, S. I., & Weisser, C. R. (2002). Breaking ground in ecocomposition: Exploring relationships between discourse and environment. *College English, 64*(5), 566–89.

Donelan, R. W., Neal, G. A., & Jones, D. L. (1994). The promise of Brown and the reality of academic grouping: The tracks of my tears. *The Journal of Negro Education, 63*(3), 376–87.

Dreeben, R. (1968). *On what is learned in schools.* Boston: Addison-Wesley.

Eisner, E. W. (1994). *The educational imagination: On the design and evaluation of school programs* (3rd ed.). New York: Macmillan.

Engels, F. (1940). *Dialectics of nature* (C. Dutt, Trans., 1st ed.). New York: International Publishers.

Engels, F. (1968). Engels to J. Bloch in Konigsberg. *Karl Marx & Frederick Engels: Their selected works* (pp. 692–93). New York: International Publishers.

Engeström, Y. (1989). The cultural-historical theory of activity and the study of political repression. *International Journal of Mental Health, 17*(4), 29–41.

Engeström, Y. (1999). Activity theory and individual and social transformation. In Y. Engeström, R. Miettinen, & R.-L. Punamaki (Eds.), *Perspectives on activity theory* (pp. 19–38). Cambridge, UK: Cambridge University Press.

Erevelles, N. (2005). Understanding curriculum as normalizing text: Disability studies meet curriculum theory. *Journal of Curriculum Studies, 37*(4), 421–39.

Fine, M. (1997). A letter to Paulo. In P. Freire, with J. W. Fraser, D. Macedo, T. McKinnon, & W. T. Stokes (Eds.), *Mentoring the mentor: A critical dialogue with Paulo Freire* (pp. 89–97). New York: Peter Lang.

Fine, M. (2006). Bearing witness: Methods for researching oppression and resistance—a textbook for critical research. *Social Justice Research, 19*(1), 83–108. doi: 10.1007/s11211-006-0001-0

Flinders, D. J., Noddings, N., & Thornton, S. J. (1986). The null curriculum: Its theoretical basis and practical implications. *Curriculum Inquiry, 16*(1), 33–42.

Foley, D. A., Levinson, B. A., & Hurtig, J. (2000). Chapter 2: Anthropology goes inside: The new educational ethnography of ethnicity and gender. *Review of Research in Education, 25*, 37–98. doi: 10.3102/0091732X025001037.

Foner, E. (2010, April 5). Twisting history in Texas. *The Nation, 290*, 4–6.

Fraser, N. (1995). From redistribution to recognition? Dilemmas of justice in a 'post-Socialist' age. *New Left Review, 212*, 68–93.

Freire, P. (1974). *Pedagogy of the oppressed* (M. B. Ramos, Trans.). New York: Seabury Press.

Freire, P. (1982a). Education as the practice of freedom (M. B. Ramos, Trans.). *Education for critical consciousness* (pp. 1–84). New York: Continuum.

Freire, P. (1982b). *Education for critical consciousness.* New York: Continuum.

Freire, P. (1982c). Extension or communication (L. Bigwood & M. Marshall, Trans.) *Education for critical consciousness* (pp. 93–164). New York: Continuum.

Freire, P. (1992). *Pedagogy of hope: Reliving pedagogy of the oppressed* (R. R. Barr, Trans., 2004 ed.). New York: Continuum.

Freire, P. (1998). *Politics and education* (P. L. Wong, Trans.). Los Angeles: UCLA Latin American Center Publications.

Freire, P., & Macedo, D. (1987). *Literacy: Reading the word and the world* (D. Macedo, Trans.). Westport, CT: Bergin & Garvey.

Freire, P., & Macedo, D. (1995). A dialogue: Culture, language, and race. *Harvard Educational Review, 65*(3), 377–402.

Gadotti, M. (1996). *Pedagogy of praxis: A dialectical philosophy of education* (J. Milton, Trans., 1st ed.). Albany: State University of New York Press.

Galeano, E. (1998). *Open veins of Latin America: Five centuries of the pillage of a continent.* New York: New York University Press.

Gamoran, A. (1992). Is ability grouping equitable? *Educational Leadership, 2*, 11–17.

Gee, J. P. (2008). *Social linguistics and literacies: Ideology in discourses* (3rd ed.). New York: RoutledgeFalmer.

Gillborn, D. (2005). Education policy as an act of white supremacy: Whiteness, critical race theory and education reform. *Journal of Education Policy, 20*(4), 485–505.

Giroux, H. A. (1980). Beyond the correspondence theory: Notes on the dynamics of educational reproduction and transformation. *Curriculum Inquiry, 10*(3), 225–47.

Glasser, H. M., & Smith III, J. P. (2008). On the vague meaning of "gender" in education research: The problem, its sources, and recommendations for practice. *Educational Researcher, 37*(6), 343–50.

Gonzalez, G. G. (1982). *Progressive education: A Marxist interpretation*. Minneapolis, MN: Marxist Educational Press.

Gramsci, A. (1971). *Selections from the prison notebooks* (Q. Hoare & G. N. Smith, Trans.). New York: International Publishers.

Greene, M. (1971). Curriculum and consciousness. *Teachers College Record, 73*(2), 253–69.

Greene, M. (1994). Chapter 10: Epistemology and educational research: The influence of recent approaches to knowledge. *Review of Research in Education, 20*, 423–64. doi: 10.3102/0091732X020001423

Gutmann, A. (1990). Democratic education in difficult times. *Teachers College Record, 92* (1), 7–20.

Hanson, D. T. (2002). Dewey's conception of an environment for teaching and learning. *Curriculum Inquiry, 32*(3), 267–80.

Haraway, D. (1991). *Simians, cyborgs, and women*. New York: Routledge.

Harden, R. M. (2001). The learning environment and the curriculum. *Medical Teacher, 23* (4), 335–36.

Harding, S. (1997). Is there a feminist model? In S. Kemp & J. Squires (Eds.), *Feminisms* (pp. 160–70). Oxford, UK: Oxford University Press.

Harding, S. (2004a). How standpoint methodology informs philosophy of science. In S. N. Hesse-Biber & P. Leavy (Eds.), *Approaches to qualitative research* (pp. 62–80). New York: Oxford University Press.

Harding, S. (2004b). Rethinking standpoint epistemology: What is "strong objectivity"? In S. Harding (Ed.), *The feminist standpoint reaader* (pp. 127–40). New York: Routledge.

Hartsock, N. C. M. (1983). The feminist standpoint: Developing the ground for a specifically feminist historical materialism. In S. Harding & M. B. Hintikka (Eds.), *Discovering reality: Feminist perspectives on epistemology, metaphysics, methodology, and philosophy of science* (pp. 283–310). Dordrecht, The Netherlands: D. Reidel.

Hartsock, N. C. M. (1998a). *The feminist standpoint revisited & other essays*. Boulder, CO: Westview Press.

Hartsock, N. C. M. (1998b). Marxist feminist dialectics for the 21st century. *Science & Society, 62*(3), 400–413.

Henry, A. (1996). Five Black women teachers critique child-centered pedagogy: Possibilities and limitations of oppositional standpoints. *Curriculum Inquiry, 26*(4), 363–84.

Hess, D. (2006). Should intelligent design be taught in social studies? *Social Education, 79* (3), 8–13.

Hess, D. (2009). *Controversy in the classroom: The democratic power of discussion*. New York: Routledge.

Hill Collins, P. (1989). The social construction of Black feminist thought. *Signs, 14*(4), 745–73.

Hirsch, E. D., Jr. (1996). *The schools we need and why we don't have them*. New York: Doubleday.

Hlebowitsh, P. S. (1993). *Radical curriculum theory reconsidered: A historical approach*. New York: Teachers College Press.

Hlebowitsh, P. S. (1997). The search for the curriculum field. *Journal of Curriculum Studies, 29*(5), 507–11.

Hlebowitsh, P. S. (1999). The burdens of the new curricularist. *Curriculum Inquiry, 29*(3), 343–54.

Hlebowitsh, P. S. (2005). Generational ideas in curriculum: A historical triangulation. *Curriculum Inquiry, 35*(1), 73–87.

Hodgkinson, H. (2002). Demographics and teacher education: An overview. *Journal of Teacher Education, 53*(2), 102–5.

Howe, K. R. (2009). Positivist dogmas, rhetoric, and the education science question. *Educational Researcher, 38*(6), 428–40. doi: 10.3102/0013189X09342003

Huebner, D. E. (1966, May 22). *The leadership role in curriculum change*. Paper presented at the Curriculum Leadership Conference, Milwaukee, Wisconsin.

Huebner, D. E. (1970, March 2). *Curriculum as the accessibility of knowledge*. Paper presented at the Curriculum Theory Study Group, Minneapolis, Minnesota.

Huebner, D. E. (1976). The moribund curriculum field: Its wake and our work. *Curriulum Inquiry, 6*(2), 153–67.

Huebner, D. E. (1999a). Curriculum as concern for man's temporality. In V. Hillis (Ed.), *The lure of the transcendent: Collected essays by Dwayne E. Huebner* (pp. 131–42). Mahwah, NJ: Lawrence Erlbaum Associates.

Huebner, D. E. (1999b). The tasks of the curricular theorist. In V. Hillis (Ed.), *The lure of the transcendent: Collected essays by Dwayne E. Huebner* (pp. 212–30). Mahwah, NJ: Lawrence Erlbaum Associates.

Hursh, D. W. (2000). Neoliberalism and the control of teachers, students, and learning: The rise of standards, standardization, and accountability. *Cultural Logic, 4*(1). Retrieved March 28, 2006, from *http://www.eserver.org/clogic/4–1/hursh.html*

Hursh, D. W., & Ross, E. W. (2000). Democratic social education: Social studies for social change. In D. W. Hursh & E. W. Ross (Eds.), *Democratic social education: Social studies for social change* (pp. 1–22). New York: Falmer Press.

Jackson, P. W. (1968). *Life in classrooms*. New York: Holt, Rinehart and Winston, Inc.

Jackson, P. W. (1980). Curriculum and its discontents. *Curriculum Inquiry, 10*(2), 159–72.

Jackson, P. W. (1996). Conceptions of curriculum and curriculum specialists. In P. W. Jackson (Ed.), *Handbook of research on curriculum: A project of the American Educational Research Association* (pp. 3–40). New York: Simon & Schuster Macmillan.

Kafala, T., & Cary, L. (2006). Postmoden moments in curriculum theory: The logic and paradox of dissensus. *Journal of Curriculum Theorizing, 22*(1), 25–43.

Kidder, W. C., & Rosner, J. (2002–3). How the SAT creates "built-in headwinds": An educational and legal analysis of disparate impact. *Santa Clara Law Review, 43,* 131–212.

Kim, P.-G., & Marshall, J. D. (2006). Synoptic curriculum texts: Representation of contemporary curriculum scholarship. *Journal of Curriculum Studies, 38*(3), 327–49.

King, L. J., Crowley, R. M., & Brown, A. L. (2010). The forgotten legacy of Carter G. Woodson: Contributions to multicultural social studies and African American history. *The Social Studies, 101*(5), 211–15. doi: 10.1080/00377990903584446

Kliebard, H. M. (1989). Problems of definition in curriculum. *Journal of Curriculum and Supervision, 5*(1), 1–5.

Kliebard, H. M. (2004). *The struggle for the American curriculum, 1893–1958* (3rd ed.). New York: RoutledgeFalmer.

Kumashiro, K. (2002). *Troubling education: Queer activism and antioppressive pedagogy*. New York: RoutledgeFalmer.

Lacey, M. (2011, January 8). Rift in Arizona as Latino class is found illegal, *The New York Times*. Retrieved January 17, from http://www.nytimes.com/2011/01/08/us/08ethnic.html?_r=1&scp=2&sq=arizona%20ethnic%20studies&st=cse

Ladson-Billings, G. (1997). Crafting a culturally relevant social studies approach. In E. W. Ross (Ed.), *The social studies curriculum: Purposes, problems, and possibilities* (pp. 121–36). Albany: State University of New York Press.

Ladson-Billings, G. (2006). From the achievement gap to the education debt: Understanding achievement in U.S. schools. *Educational Researcher, 35*(7), 3–12.

Ladson-Billings, G., & Tate IV, W. F. (1995). Towards a critical race theory of education. *Teachers College Record, 97*(1), 47–68.

Laird, J., Lew, S., DeBell, M., & Chapman, C. (2006). *Dropout rates in the United States: 2002 and 2003* (p. 68). Washington, DC: U.S. Department of Education: National Center for Education Statistics.

Landau, I. (2008). Problems with feminist standpoint theory in science education. *Science & Education, 17,* 1081–88. doi: 10.1007/s11191-007-9131-5

Lather, P. (1992). Post-critical pedagogies: A feminist reading. In C. Luke & J. Gore (Eds.), *Feminisms and critical pedagogy* (pp. 120–37). New York: Routledge.

Lee, E., Menkhart, D., & Okazawa-Rey, M. (Eds.). (1998). *Beyond heroes and holidays.* Washington, DC: Network of Educators on the Americas.

Leont'ev, A. N. (1981). The problem of activity in psychology. In J. V. Wertsch (Ed.), *The concept of activity in Soviet psychology* (pp. 37–71). New York: M.E. Sharpe Inc.

Levine, D. (2000). Carter G. Woodson and the Afrocentrists: Common foes of mis-education. *The High School Journal, 84*(1), 5–13.

Lipman, P. (2004). *High stakes education: Inequality, globalization, and urban school reform.* NewYork: RoutledgeFalmer.

Lippi-Green, R. (2011). *English with an accent: Language, ideology, and discrimination in the United States.* New York: Routledge.

Lucas, S. R. (1999). *Tracking inequality: Stratification and mobility in American high schools* (1st ed.). New York: Teachers College Press.

Lukacs, G. (1971). *History and class consciousness.* Cambridge, MA: MIT Press.

Luke, C., & Gore, J. (Eds.). (1992). *Feminisms and critical pedagogy.* New York: Routledge.

Manicom, A. (1992). Feminist pedagogy: Transformations, standpoints, and politics. *Canadian Journal of Education, 17*(3), 365–89.

Margolis, E., Soldatenko, M., Acker, S., & Gair, M. (2001). Peekaboo: Hiding and outing the curriculum. In E. Margolis (Ed.), *The hidden curriculum in higher education* (pp. 1–22). New York: Routledge.

Marri, A. R. (2005). Building a framework for classroom-based multicultural democratic education: Learning from three skilled teachers. *Teachers College Record, 107*(5), 1036–59.

Marx, K., & Engels, F. (1956). *The holy family or critique of critical critique.* Moscow: Foreign Languages Publishing House.

Marx, K., & Engels, F. (1978). The German ideology: Part I. In R. C. Tucker (Ed.), *The Marx-Engels reader* (pp. 146–200). New York: W.W. Norton & Company.

McCarthy, C. (1990). Multicultural education, minority identities, textbooks, and the challenge of curriculum reform. *Journal of Education, 172*(2), 118–29.

McKinley Jr., J. C. (2010, March 12). Texas conservatives win curriculum change, *The New York Times*. Retrieved November 17, 2010, from http://www.nytimes.com/2010/03/13/education/13texas.html

McLaren, P., & Farahmandpur, R. (2005). *Teaching against global capitalism and the new imperialism: A critical pedagogy.* New York: Rowman and Littlefield Publishers.

McNeil, L. M. (2000). *Contradictions of school reform: Educational costs of standardized testing.* New York: Routledge.

Menkhart, D., Murray, A. D., & View, J. L. (Eds.). (2004). *Putting the movement back into civil rights teaching.* Washington, DC: Teaching for Change.

Miller, J. L. (2005). The American curriculum field and its worldly encounters. *Journal of Curriculum Theorizing, 21*(2), 9–24.

Morais, A. M. (2002). Basil Bernstein at the micro level of the classroom. *British Journal of Sociology of Education, 23*(4), 559–69.

Morrison, K. R. B. (2004). The poverty of curriculum theory: A critique of Wraga and Hlebowitsh. *Journal of Curriculum Studies, 36*(4), 487–94.

Natriello, G., & Pallas, A. M. (2001). The development and impact of high-stakes testing. In G. Orfield & M. L. Kornhaber (Eds.), *Raising standards or raising barriers? Inequality and high-stakes testing in public education* (pp. 19–38). New York: Century Foundation Press.

Ngugi, W. T. (1986). *Decolonising the mind: The politics of language in African literature.* Portsmouth, NH: Heinemann.

Nichols, S. L., & Berliner, D. C. (2007). *Collateral damage: How high-stakes testing corrupts America's schools.* Cambridge, MA: Harvard Education Press.

Oakes, J. (2005). *Keeping track: How schools structure inequality* (2nd ed.). New Haven, CT: Yale University Press.

Oakes, J., Welner, K., Yonezawa, S., & Allen, R. L. (1998). Norms and politics of equity-minded change: Researching the "zone of mediation". In M. Fullan (Ed.), *International handbook of educational change* (pp. 953–75). Norwell, MA: Kluer Academic Publishers.

Ollman, B. (2003). *Dance of the dialectic: Steps in Marx's method* (1st ed.). Chicago: University of Illinois Press.

Parker, W. (2005). Teaching against idiocy. *Phi Delta Kappan,* 344–51.

Perry, M. (2002). *Marxism and history.* New York: Palgrave.

Peterson, B. (2001). Rethinking the U.S. Constitutional Convention: A role play. In B. Bigelow, B. Harvey, S. Karp, & L. Miller (Eds.), *Rethinking our classrooms volume 2: Teaching for equity and social justice* (pp. 63–69). Milwaukee, WI: Rethinking Schools Ltd.

Pinar, W. F. (1978). The reconceptualization of curriculum studies. *Curriculum Studies, 10* (3), 205–14.

Pinar, W. F. (1998). Introduction. In W. F. Pinar (Ed.), *Curriculum: Toward new identities* (pp. ix-xxxiv). New York: Garland Publishing.

Pinar, W. F. (1999). Response: Gracious submission. *Educational Researcher, 28*(1), 14–15.

Pinar, W. F. (2006). Relocating cultural studies into curriculum studies. *Journal of Curriculum Theorizing, 22*(2), 55–72.

Pinar, W. F. (Ed.). (1975). *Curriculum theorizing: The reconceptualists.* Berkeley, CA: McCutchan Publishing.

Pinar, W. F., Reynolds, W. M., Slattery, P., & Taubman, P. M. (1995). *Understanding curriculum: An introduction to the study of historical and contemporary curriculum discourses.* New York: Peter Lang.

Pinnick, C. L. (2008). Science education for women: Situated cognition, feminist standpoint theory, and the status of women in science. *Science & Education, 17,* 1055–63. doi: 10.1007/s11191-008-9153-7

Popkewitz, T. S., & Fendler, L. (Eds.). (1999). *Critical theories in education: Changing terrains of knowledge and politics.* New York: Routledge.

Roberts, P. (2003). Knowledge, dialogue, and humanization: Exploring Freire's philosophy. In M. Peters, C. Lankshear, & M. Olssen (Eds.), *Critical theory and the human condition: Founders and praxis* (pp. 169–83). New York: Peter Lang.

Rodriguez, R. C. (2010). 'Greco-Roman knowledge only' in Arizona schools: Indigenous wisdom outlawed once again. *Rethinking Schools, 24*(4), 49–51.

Rosenbaum, J. E. (1976). *Making inequality: The hidden curriculum of high school tracking.* New York: John Wiley & Sons.

Säfström, C. A. (1999). On the way to a postmodern curriculum theory—moving from the question of unity to the question of difference. *Studies in Philosophy of Education, 18* (4), 221–33.

Sandoval, C. (2000). *Methodology of the oppressed.* Minneapolis: University of Minnesota Press.

Sayers, S. (1990). Marxism and the dialectical method: A critique of G.A. Cohen. In S. Sayers & P. Osborne (Eds.), *Socialism, feminism, and philosophy: A radical philosophy reader* (pp. 140–68). New York: Routledge.

Schwab, J. J. (1969). The practical: a language for curriculum. *School Review, 78*(1), 1–23.

Scott, E. C., & Branch, G. (Eds.). (2006). *Not in our classrooms: Why intelligent design is wrong for our schools.* Boston: Beacon Press.

Scribner, S. (1997). Mind in action: A functional approach to thinking. In M. Cole, Y. Engestrom, & O. Vasquez (Eds.), *Mind, culture, and activity: Seminal papers from the laboratory of comparative human cognition* (pp. 354–68). Cambridge, UK: Cambridge University Press.

Shook, J. R. (2000). *Dewey's empirical theory of knowledge and reality*. Nashville, TN: Vanderbilt University Press.

Shor, I. (1992). *Empowering education: Critical teaching for social change* (1st ed.). Chicago: The University of Chicago Press.

Shor, I., & Freire, P. (1987). *A pedagogy for liberation: Dialogues on transforming education*. South Hadley, MA: Bergin & Garvey Publishers.

Shorto, R. (2010, February 14). Founding father? *The New York Times*. Retrieved November 16, 2010, from http://www.nytimes.com/2010/02/14/magazine/14texbooks-t.html

Siegel, H. (2006). Epistemological diversity and educational research: Much ado about nothing much? *Educational Researcher, 35*(3), 3–12. doi: 10.3102/0013189X035002003

Sirin, S. R. (2005). Socioeconomic status and student achievement: A meta-analytic review of research. *Review of Educational Research, 75*(3), 417–53.

Slabbert, J. A., & Hattingh, A. (2006). 'Where is the post-modern truth we have lost in reductionist knowledge?': A curriculum's epitaph. *Journal of Curriculum Studies, 38*(6), 701–18.

Slattery, P. (2006). *Curriculum development in the postmodern era* (2nd ed.). New York: Routledge.

Sleeter, C. (2000–2001). Epistemological diversity in research on preservice teacher preparation for historically underserved children. *Review of Research in Education, 25*, 209–50.

Sleeter, C. (2002). State curriculum standards and the shaping of student consciousness. *Social Justice, 29*(4), 8–25.

Sleeter, C. E. (2004). Standardizing imperialism. *Rethinking Schools, 19*(1), 26–30.

Sleeter, C. E., & Stillman, J. (2005). Standardizing knowledge in a multicultural society. *Curriculum Inquiry, 35*(1), 27–46.

Smith, B. D. (1985). John Dewey's theory of consciousness. *Educational Theory, 35*(3), 267–72.

Spatig, L. (2005). Feminist critique of developmentalism: What's in it for teachers? *Theory and Research in Education, 3*(3), 299–326. doi: 10.1177/1477878505057431

Stables, A. (2005). Multiculturalism and moral education: Individual positioning, dialogue, and cultural practice. *Journal of Moral Education, 34*(2), 185–97.

Steenland, K. (1974). The coup in Chile. *Latin American Perspectives, 1*(2), 9–29.

Takacs, D. (2002). Postitionality, epistemology, and social justice in the classroom. *Social Justice 29*(4), 168–81.

Teitelbaum, K. (1988). Contestation and curriculum: The efforts of American socialists, 1900–920. In L. E. Beyer & M. W. Apple (Eds.), *The curriculum: Problems, politics, and possibilities* (pp. 32–55). Albany: State University of New York Press.

Teitelbaum, K. (1991). Critical lessons from our past: Curricula of Socialist Sunday schools in the United States. In M. W. Apple & L. K. Christian-Smith (Eds.), *The politics of the textbook* (pp. 135–65). New York: Routledge.

Valenzuela, A. (2005a). Accountability and the privatization agenda. In A. Valenzuela (Ed.), *Leaving children behind: How 'Texas style' accountability fails Latino youth* (pp. 263–94). New York: State University of New York Press.

Valenzuela, A. (Ed.). (2005b). *Leaving children behind: How 'Texas style' accountability fails Latino youth*. New York: State University of New York Press.

van Merrienboer, J. J. G., & Paas, F. (2003). Powerful learning and the many faces of instructional design: Toward a framework for the design of powerful learning environments. In E. De Corte & European Association for Learning and Instruction. (Eds.), *Powerful learning environments: Unravelling basic components and dimensions* (pp. 3–19). Oxford, UK: Pergamon.

Vavrus, M. (2002). *Transforming the multicultural education of teachers: Theory, research and practice* (1st ed.). New York: Teachers College Press.

Virginia State Board of Education. (1943). *Course of study for Virginia elementary schools: Grades I-VII* (Vol. XXV, No. 6). Richmond, VI: Division of Purchase and Printing.

Volosinov, V. N. (1986). *Marxism and the philosophy of language* (L. Matejka & I. R. Titunik, Trans.). Cambridge, MA: Harvard University Press.

Vygotsky, L. S. (1929). The problem of the cultural development of the child. *Journal of Genetic Psychology: Child Behavior, Animal Behavior, and Comparative Psychology, XXXVI*(1), 415–34.

Vygotsky, L. S. (1981). The genesis of higher mental functions (J. V. Wertsch, Trans.). In J. V. Wertsch (Ed.), *The concept of activity in Soviet psychology* (pp. 144–88). Armonk, NY: M.E. Sharpe.

Vygotsky, L. S. (1987). Thinking and speech (N. Minick, Trans.). In R. W. Rieber & A. Carton (Eds.), *The collected works of L.S. Vygotsky: Problems of general psychology including the volume thinking and speech* (Vol. 1, pp. 37–285). New York: Plenum Press.

Wallat, C., & Green, J. (1979). Social rules and communication contexts in kindergarten. *Theory Into Practice, 18*(4), 275–84.

Watkins, W. H. (1993). Black curriculum orientations: A preliminary inquiry. *Harvard Educational Review, 63*(3), 321–38.

Wei, D., & Kamel, R. (Eds.). (1998). *Resistance in paradise: Rethinking 100 years of U.S. involvement in the Caribbean and the Pacific.* Philadelphia: American Friends Service Committee.

Weiler, K. (1991). Freire and a feminist pedagogy of difference. *Harvard Educational Review, 61*(4), 449–74.

Weisz, E. (1989). A view of curriculum as opportunities to learn: An examination of curriculum enactment. *Education, 107*(2), 155–161.

Willis, P. (1977). *Learning to labor: How working class kids get working class jobs.* New York: Columbia University Press.

Wise, T. (2008). *Speaking treason fluently: Anti-racist reflections from an angry white male.* Berkeley, CA: Soft Skull Press.

Wise, T. (2010, May 4, 2010). *On illegal people … and forgetful ones: Reflections on race, nation and immigration.* Retrieved September 28, 2010, from http://www.timwise.org/2010/05/on-illegal-people-and-forgetful-ones-reflections-on-race-nation-and-immigration/

Wong, T.-H., & Apple, M. W. (2003). Rethinking the education-state formation connection: The state, cultural struggles, and changing the school. In M. W. Apple (Ed.), *The state and the politics of knowledge* (pp. 81–107). New York: Routledge.

Woods, A., & Grant, T. (2002). *Reason in revolt: Dialectical philosophy and modern science.* New York: Algora Publishing.

Woodson, C. G. (1990/1933). *The mis-education of the negro.* Trenton, NJ: Africa World Press, Inc.

Woodson, C. G., & Wesley, C. H. (1959/1933). *The story of the Negro retold.* Washington, DC: The Associated Publishers.

Wraga, W. G. (1998). Interesting, if true: Historical perspectives on the 'reconceptualization' of curriculum studies. *Journal of Curriculum and Supervision, 14*(1), 5–28.

Wraga, W. G. (1999). 'Extracting sun-beams out of cucumbers': The retreat from practice in reconceptualized curriculum studies. *Educational Researcher, 28*(1), 4–13.

Wraga, W. G., & Hlebowitsh, P. S. (2003). Toward a renaissance in curriculum theory and development in the USA. *Journal of Curriculum Studies, 35*(4), 425–37.

Yang, K. W. (2009). Mathematics, critical literacy, and youth participatory action research. *New Directions for Youth Development, (123),* 99–118. doi: 10.1002/yd.317

Yang, K. W., & Duncan-Andrade, J. (2005). *Doc Ur Block.* Retrieved June 26, 2009, from http://www.edliberation.org/resources/records/doc-ur-block

Yonezawa, S. (2000). Unpacking the black box of tracking decisions: Critical tales of families navigating the course placement process. In M. G. Sanders (Ed.), *Schooling students placed at risk: Research, policy, and practice in the education of poor and minority adolescents* (pp. 109–37). Mahwah, NJ: Lawrence Erlbaum.

Zinchenko, V. P. (1996). Developing activity theory: The zone of proximal development and beyond. In B. A. Nardi (Ed.), *Context and consciousness: Activity theory and human-computer interaction* (pp. 283–324). Cambridge, MA: The MIT Press.

Zinn, H. (1995). *A people's history of the United States: 1492-present* (Rev. and updated ed.). New York: HarperPerennial.

AUTHOR BIOGRAPHY

Wayne Au is an assistant professor in the Education Program at the University of Washington, Bothell Campus, and he is an editor and regular contributor to the social justice teacher magazine, *Rethinking Schools*. Au has published widely in the areas of critical education theory, critical educational policy studies, and teaching for social justice, and he is author of *Unequal By Design: High-Stakes Testing and the Standardization of Inequality* (Routledge, 2009), editor of *Rethinking Multicultural Education: Teaching for Racial and Cultural Justice* (Rethinking Schools, 2009), and co-editor of *The Routledge International Handbook of Critical Education* (Routledge, 2010).

INDEX

unofficial curriculum 32; Weisz's social
curriculum 32
Connell, R. W. 60, 69
consciousness: and curriculum 91–5;
relative autonomy of schools and 19,
26, 95–8; *see also* critical consciousness;
dialectical conception of consciousness
Cooper, C. W. 59
Counts, G. S. 68, 72
*Course of Study for Virginia Elementary
Schools: Grades I-VII* 76–8
critical consciousness 16, 24–6, 27, 68; and
curriculum 91–5; development of 73,
76, 81, 82, 84, 88, 99–101; relative
autonomy of schools and 19, 26, 95–8
critical praxis 25–6
critical reflection 24–6
"curricular justice" 60
curricular resistance 2–3
curricular standpoint: of benefit to
curricular studies 68–70, 98, 99;
contemporary examples 78–88; *Course
of Study for Virginia Elementary Schools:
Grades I-VII* 76–8; and curricular
knowledge 66, 67, 71, 72; development
of critical consciousness 73, 76, 81, 82,
84, 88, 99–101; English education/
language arts 78–80; examples of
72–89; framework for 65–7, 71–2;
historical examples 72–8; links to
dialectical conception of consciousness
67–8, 89, 98; mathematics examples
82–7; power relations and 66, 71, 78,
89, 92; science education 80–2, 88;
social relations and 66, 67, 68, 71, 79,
88, 89; social studies/history education
87–8; socialist Sunday schools 72–3; and
understanding material realities 57, 64,
65, 67, 70, 89, 98; Woodson's retelling
of African American history 73–6
"curriculum accords" 65
curriculum-as-tool: in activity of accessing
knowledge 39–41; pedagogic discourse
and practical classroom examples of
41–4; power relations in structure and
accessibility of knowledge 45–9, 92;
standardized testing 44–5
curriculum studies: benefits of curricular
standpoint theory to 68–70, 98, 99;
crisis in 3–4, 32; critical turn in 4–5, 7;
criticisms of pragmatic and subjective
considerations 6–8; importance of 11;
and importance of theory 16; and need

for an increased focus on practice 7,
8–9; pragmatic/positivist paradigm 5–6;
"reconceptualization" of 4; subjective/
postmodern paradigm 4–5, 7–8
curriculum tracking 46

D
Dagbovie, P. G. 73, 74, 75
Davis, R. 15, 23, 24, 68
Dean, J. 80, 81, 82
DeLissovoy, N. 60, 61, 62
Democracy and Education 34
design of educational environments 35–9;
art/creativity 37; capital investment 35;
and conceptions of educational
environments 37–8; and concepts of
curriculum as knowledge embodied in
environmental form 38–9, 44, 92; and
connection to dialectical conception of
consciousness 39; materials 35; people
35–6; social policy 37; symbols 35;
temporality 36–7
Dewey, J. 23, 30, 33–4, 49
dialectical conception of consciousness:
being and knowing 17–18, 19, 26, 67;
and being conscious of consciousness
22–4, 26; and critical reflection 24–6;
curricular standpoint and links to 67–8,
89, 98; design of educational
environments and connections to 39;
materialism 18–19; praxis 19, 39;
relative autonomy of schools and
consciousness 19, 26, 95–8; social
consciousness 21–2, 26; and use of tools
20, 39–40
Dreeben, R. 31

E
economic self-determination 85, 86
educational politics: critical turn in 4;
impact of evangelical Christianity on
92–5; struggle against regressive 24, 62–5
educational research and standpoint theory
58–62; progressive curriculum politics
62–5
Eisner, E. W. 30, 31
enacted curriculum 31–2
Engels, F. 9.26, 18, 20, 39, 51, 52, 67, 97
English education/language arts 78–80
environmental design: curriculum as a
problem of complex 33–5; *see also*
design of educational environments
Erlandson, D. A. 58, 61

student consciousness in 92; Texas Board of Education (TBE) review of 93–5
socialist Sunday schools 72–3
Solomon, J. 46
Spatig, L. 58
Stables, A. 62, 63
standardized testing 44–5
standpoint theory 9–10, 52–5, 72–3; application in "antioppressive education" 59–60; argument for multicultural education in schools 64–5; curricular standpoint framework 65–7, 71–2; in educational research 58–62; epistemology and strong objectivity 55–8, 64, 72; and feminism 53, 56, 58, 61, 68, 70, 83; power relations and 9–10, 53, 54–5, 56, 69; and progressive education 62–5; social location and 55–7, 65, 66, 69, 89
The Story of the Negro Retold 74
Sunday schools, socialist 72–3

T
Takacs, D. 59
"The Tasks of the Curricular Theorist" 35
Teitelbaum, K. 72, 73
testing, standardized 44–5
Texas Board of Education (TBE) 93–5
textbooks: to challenge scientific racism 74–5; evangelical Christian influence on shaping of 93, 94–5

thinking about thinking 22–4, 26
tools and consciousness 20, 39–40, 67; *see also* curriculum-as-tool
tracking 46–9, 58

U
Unequal by Design 10
unofficial curriculum 32
U.S. Constitutional Convention 87–8

V
Virginia Elementary Schools' course of study 76–8
volition 24, 26
Vygotsky, L. S. 9, 16, 18, 20, 21, 23, 24, 25, 26, 29, 39, 40, 44, 49, 67, 68, 97

W
Watkins, W. H. 59
Weisz, E. 31, 32
Wesley, C. H. 74
Woodson, C. G. 73–6
World Trade Organization 2–3, 99–101
Wraga, W. G. 4, 5, 6, 7, 8

Y
Yang, K. W. 68, 84, 85, 86
Yonezawa, S. 47, 58

Z
Zinn, H. 2, 24

Unequal
By Design

**High-Stakes
Testing and the
Standardization
of Inequality**

CPSIA information can be obtained
at www.ICGtesting.com
Printed in the USA
BVHW080521051218
534695BV00001B/42/P